MW00912423

Some early praise for Jim Joseph's new book, **The Experience Effect for Small Business***:*

"This easy-to-read marketing book delivers insights into how small businesses can build their brand while creating strong connections to customers without requiring the big advertising budgets typically found in Fortune 500 companies. It's a must-read, and Jim's practical approach to marketing is full of useful concepts and strategies that are easily adaptive to all types of small businesses."
Renee L. Harris, Chair and Academic Director, New York University

"Jim's wisdom for building my consulting practice has been invaluable. In a world of books that champion big budget solutions for big corporations, Jim focuses on the small business owner with smart, inexpensive approaches to building a real brand experience that will grow sales."
Mark Schnurman, President of Filament, Inc

"No doubt this book will challenge and help shift the mindset of many small businesses. Using examples we all relate to, Joseph makes his points with clarity and relevance. The book is most enjoyable AND engaging...unlike any other marketing book I've read (except the original "The Experience Effect"!). Can't wait to use it in my next marketing class at St. Joseph's University!"
Laura L. Barry, Entrepreneur and Adjunct Professor

"I wish I had this book when I had my own small business. It would have made me think differently about my customers, and would have helped me avoid making costly mistakes."
Karen Fossedal, Owner, Singer Sewing of Aiken, SC

The Experience Effect for Small Business

Big Brand Results with
Small Business Resources

By Jim Joseph
Author of the award-winning
The Experience Effect
http://JimJosephExp.com

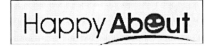

20660 Stevens Creek Blvd., Suite 210
Cupertino, CA 95014

Published by Happy About®
20660 Stevens Creek Blvd., Suite 210, Cupertino, CA 95014
http://happyabout.com

First Printing: January 2012
Hardcover ISBN: 978-1-60005-206-4 (1-60005-206-1)
eBook ISBN: 978-1-60005-209-5 (1-60005-209-6)
Place of Publication: Silicon Valley, California, USA
Hardcover Library of Congress Number: 2011942256

Trademarks

Warning and Disclaimer

iv

Dedication

This book is dedicated to Christopher, remembering the amazing journey we had with our small business, and to Alicia and JP who are embarking on their own journeys—may all of our experiences bring great joy!

A Message from Happy About®

Thank you for your purchase of this Happy About book. It is available online at http://happyabout.info/experienceeffectsmallbusiness.php or at other online and physical bookstores.

- Please contact us for quantity discounts at sales@happyabout.info
- If you want to be informed by email of upcoming Happy About® books, please email bookupdate@happyabout.info

Happy About is interested in you if you are an author who would like to submit a non-fiction book proposal or a corporation that would like to have a book written for you. Please contact us by email at editorial@happyabout.info or phone (1-408-257-3000).

Other Happy About books available include:

- Red Fire Branding:
  http://www.happyabout.com/redfirebranding.php
- Storytelling About Your Brand Online & Offline:
  http://www.happyabout.com/storytelling.php
- 42 Rules of Social Media for Small Business:
  http://www.happyabout.com/42rules/social-media-business.php
- Social Media Success!:
  http://www.happyabout.com/social-media-success.php
- #SOCIAL MEDIA PR tweet Book01:
  http://www.happyabout.com/thinkaha/socialmediaprtweet01.php
- 42 Rules for Driving Success With Books:
  http://www.happyabout.com/42rules/books-drive-success.php
- 42 Rules to Increase Sales Effectiveness:
  http://happyabout.com/42rules/increasesaleseffectiveness.php
- Managing Salespeople:
  http://www.happyabout.com/managingsalespeople.php
- I'm at a Networking Event—Now What???:
  http://www.happyabout.com/networking-event.php
- I'm on LinkedIn—Now What??? (3rd Edition):
  http://www.happyabout.com/linkedinhelp.php
- 42 Rules for Effective Connections:
  http://www.happyabout.com/42rules/effectiveconnections.php
- I Need a Killer Press Release—Now What???:
  http://www.happyabout.com/killer-press-release.php

Acknowledgments

Bringing a book to market is a tremendous amount of work—no author does it alone. When my first book came out, it was a defining moment in my life. I was so happy to get my voice "recorded!" The reception my book received was over-whelming. The thought of doing it twice is mind-boggling, but here we are!

I want to thank everyone in my life for their encouragement and support for me these past few years. It has meant the world to me.

My team at Lippe Taylor—for their undying creativity, each and every day.

My students at NYU—for the inspiration to keep learning.

All of my colleagues through the years—for the give and take and "therapy sessions."

My new friends at Happy About—for working so hard and putting up with me.

Family and Friends—for the motivation to keep doing it.

Contents

Behind the Book
So I Got to Thinking…

"There's really no reason why a small business can't perform like a big brand, and no reason why it can't have the same kind of successes."

I'm a marketing guy. Always have been and always will be, I suppose.

I look at everything through the lens of marketing—I just can't help myself. I knew from day one that I wanted to "do" marketing, so I spent my entire career honing my craft by making sure I got experience working on a variety of brands, in a mix of categories, across a range of consumer targets. I can't say that I've seen it all, but there are days when it certainly feels like it.

Yes, I'm one of those people who knew at a young age what I wanted to do. I'm not sure I even knew what marketing was back then, but I knew that somehow, someway it was for me.

I would watch the television commercials more than the actual shows, and I would read the print ads more than the actual articles in magazines. I just loved all the brands and what they had to say.

Maybe it was the Faberge "and she told two friends" commercial from the 1980's that really did it for me, I'm not sure. The commercial had me hooked without possibly knowing it was foreshadowing today's social marketing and Facebook! See, that's how I think.

Right after college I went into sales at the then Carnation Company, because all of my trusted advisors at the time told me that if I wanted to go into marketing, then I had better get some sales experience.

I then went to grad school at Columbia, and while at school, I joined the classic Johnson's Baby Products Company. I blossomed, and quickly became a bit of a new products expert. I launched a portfolio of new products at various divisions of Johnson & Johnson—seven new products in five years, to be exact.

Later in my career, I got bit by the entrepreneurial bug and started my own agency. I can't believe I had the guts to do it, but I saw an opportunity in the market and I seized it. This little agency was among the first to start building brand websites back in the day, and we were on top of the world.

We were a super smart and creative team doing just what entrepreneurs should be doing—good work. I then sold this agency to The Publicis Groupe, and got the chance to help even more clients solve their marketing

challenges by running agencies that specialized in promotional marketing, direct marketing, digital marketing, and of course
advertising. Marketing, marketing, marketing—I can't say it enough.

After many brand assignments, many
agency mergers, and lots of agency
reinvention and rebranding, I finally wrote
my first book in 2010 called *The Experience
Effect*. It is really a compilation of all my
marketing experiences, and it helped me
commit to paper what good marketing is all
about and how to do it well.

My book drew an incredibly positive
response from the industry, including a
Silver Medal at the Axiom Business Book
Awards for Best Marketing Book of the year.
I was thrilled beyond belief.

The Experience Effect discusses how
creating a relevant brand experience can
have a tremendous effect on your customers
and on your business.

The "funny" thing is that I was writing that
book just as the economy started to unravel
around all of us. People were losing jobs left
and right, and many people found themselves stuck. Stuck in a place they either
didn't want to be in or stuck in a place that
they didn't realize would become so long
term.

Raises disappeared, bonuses evaporated,
and promotions were long put on hold.
Careers stalled and we were all standing in

place. If we wanted to keep moving forward, we had to start thinking differently. Perhaps the tried and true just didn't work anymore?

Many of us still find ourselves turning away from the expected, and counting on our own skills and experiences to make a living. Entrepreneurism is still on the rise, as America looks to Americans for our own recovery and growth.

Small businesses are growing again.

I can feel it all around me. As I go on speaking engagements, I am constantly being asked how big brand marketing principles can be applied to small businesses. It's so important as we see small businesses becoming the backbone of our economy once more. We need to support small businesses any way possible.

So I got to thinking ...

Running a small business is so much easier said than done. It's really hard work and it feels like we are often in it alone. Most small business owners lack the resources they need to truly accomplish their goals and to maximize their potential.

They look longingly at the big brands and the big corporations, wishing that they were able to replicate their marketing power and longing for those big successes. Many of these small business owners do get there eventually, but all of us could use some help.

So I decided to write a sequel to *The Experience Effect* that would be dedicated to helping small business owners become successful by creating a brand experience for their customers.

The Experience Effect for Small Business.

In this book I hope to give small business owners the kind of marketing knowledge they need to succeed like a big brand, despite more limited resources. There's really no reason why a small business can't perform like a big brand, and no reason why it can't have the same kind of successes. It's just that so many don't know how because they don't have the specific marketing education, skills, or experience, nor the same size budgets or access to resources.

My hope is that this book will give an inside peek at how big mega brands do marketing so that you can do what's appropriate for your size business. I hope to give you the tools to build your own Experience Effect for your own small business!

The book begins by talking about how important an incredible brand experience is to our customers and to our business's success.

We will walk through the steps necessary to build an Experience Effect for our customers, much like what the big brands do, but for small business. I will show how to replicate big brand activities on limited budgets, and with far fewer resources.

We will learn by example to serve as inspiration, because we can learn a lot by watching the work of other brands in the marketplace. I love seeing and learning what other brands do, and I write about it everyday on my blog at JimJosephExp.com.

It is my goal to help small businesses, the backbone of our American economy, become just as successful as big businesses. I want to give small businesses access to some of the knowledge and methodologies that are used to create powerful marketing programs.

These tools will ultimately create a compelling brand experience for their customers and will keep them coming back, time and time again.

Let's get started.

Start by Observing
Inspired by Tom

"Start paying more attention to marketing activity, from big brands and small."

I have been in marketing for a long time now, and I have to say that it doesn't get any easier. It's tough work. Just when we think we've got it conquered, something new comes along to prove that we really don't know what we're talking about. The world may take a cultural shift and radically change peoples' attitudes and behaviors—like social media, or an economic meltdown, or a natural disaster, or a big new trend in pop culture.

When we're in marketing, we need to expect it to be a never-ending job. The minute we have our plan in place, something changes—like when a new competitor enters the market, or when new government legislation changes the rules of the road, or when a new technological advance requires a rethink.

This is true of big business and it is certainly true of small. Nothing stays the same and it is a tireless and ever changing job.

The minute we are feeling safe and secure, something comes along to rock our world. Our work is never done, although as a small business owner you have a much quicker ability to react, and probably a better ability to capitalize on those constant changes.

That's what keeps me going, to tell you the truth. I love the business world and I love marketing. Just when I think I am getting bored, along comes a new marketing program that completely captivates me. Like a new charity program with American Express and the television show Glee or a new line of skin care products that promises to erase the signs of aging differently.

My first piece of advice is to start paying more attention to marketing activity, from big brands and small. From television advertising, to social media, to websites, to instore displays, observe how brands attempt to connect with their customers, and the language that they use.

Check out the incentive offers that encourage purchases, and the creativity that brands put out there to attract attention. Sign up for Facebook updates and Twitter posts and read what the brands are saying. You'll be amazed at what you can learn and what you can apply to your own business.

One of the biggest compliments I receive from my first book is that people tell me how they notice "marketing" more than ever now. They find themselves analyzing Applebee's, Whole Foods, and Chase in addition to small restaurants, retail stores, and services. They now pay more attention to the marketing of brands and are enjoying it.

They also pay particularly close attention to the experience they are having when they walk into a store or restaurant, and whether they really like it or not. They are reading print advertisements more carefully and really paying attention to brands on Twitter and Facebook.

You should start doing the same.

Some of the marketing activity will surprise you. Take the home paint category—it is incredibly competitive. The "paint wars" between Benjamin Moore, Behr, and Sherwin-Williams (to name just a few) is fascinating to watch, and very creative. Color matchers, smart phone apps, cans that are easy to pour, partnerships with HGTV—the marketing activity and the brand experiences go on and on.

Get inspired by what's in the marketplace. It will help create new ideas for customers and it will keep the business fresh. A key ingredient to being a good marketer is to stay on the pulse of pop culture and consumer behavior.

Marketing is certainly hard work but it's also in large part about being inspired by what's around you: part perspiration and part inspiration. Great marketing involves being inspired by what's in the marketplace already, and then giving your own customers an experience to stay engaged in the brand.

Brands should be inspiring, and that should be the goal for your small business.

Since you run a small business, you may not think that you can be inspirational, but you couldn't be more wrong. Small businesses are the backbone of our economy and our way of life, and you truly have the opportunity to add real value to people's lives more so than most large consumer products.

Plus it's never too early to get ready to be big!

Take a look at Facebook—a tiny little idea from a couple of kids in college. It started out very small, and grew to be a huge force in pop culture, radically changing the way that people of all ages and backgrounds communicate with each other and stay in each other's lives.

What started out as a small idea became a cultural revolution and a very big business.

The founders of Facebook had an idea, and an insight about how people wanted to join communities. They had big aspirations even though they didn't start out with big budgets. They turned a small business idea into a life-changing experience.

The guys that started Facebook were not the first entrepreneurs to create a pop culture phenomenon that ultimately changed our behavior.

Take a look at the fast food category. The history of McDonald's is another stellar example of a simple concept that slowly grew to international success. Two brothers started a small burger joint, which later became a national chain that invented consistent mass production in food service. Over a billion sold, right?

They too turned a small business idea into a big business fortune.

But it's not just about being big. Some brands stay small but their impact is still huge. Tom's Shoes is a relatively small company with a very cool concept: for every pair of shoes sold, another pair goes to a child in need. Will Tom's Shoes ever be Nike or Cole Haan? Probably not, but it's a small brand with a big idea and a huge impact. Tom's Shoes is now expanding to the sunglass industry, with the same core concept.

It's also important to point out that Tom's has also inspired other brands to include cause marketing in their brand experience. It comes up in brainstorm sessions at my agency all the time.

Skechers did an out right copy with their brand Bob's: for every pair of Bob's shoes sold, a pair goes to a child in need. Imitation is the greatest form of flattery I guess.

There is no reason why small businesses can't have big aspirations. It comes with the territory, really. Innovation and creativity doesn't come from the burearacy of big businesses, it comes from the entrepreneurialism of small businesses.

So run with it, and I hope this book helps.

As you read through the chapters in this book, take note of examples of influential brands that have changed the world, or certainly their corner of it.

You too can do the same, just by creating an amazing brand experience for customers. I will illustrate how to do this, step by step.

In Chapter One, we will talk about what marketing is all about, whether big or small. Many people who have never taken a marketing course in their lives are finding themselves doing marketing. Here, I will welcome you to the wonderful world of marketing.

In Chapter Two, we will talk about how your business is a brand. Thinking like a brand will open a range of opportunities, and it's the emotional connection with customers that makes it all happen.

I believe that good marketing is about creating a powerful and compelling brand experience for the customer. In Chapter Three, we will define the Experience Effect and show how it helps elevate the brand.

Chapter Four will show you that the first step in creating a brand experience is making sure that we have a really good grasp of what our brand is all about. We'll need to define the kind of business we are in, and the kind of brand we want to be, now and years into the future.

Part of defining the brand is understanding the competition. In Chapter Five, I hope to give a different perspective on the competition by forcing us to think more broadly. Then we'll draw some concentric circles that will change how we look at our competition.

In Chapter Six, we will finally turn to our customers. Great marketing begins and ends with our customers, so here we will start to put some definition around who they are and what makes them tick.

Identifying the customer is only half the battle. The challenge is getting to know them better than anyone else. In Chapter Seven, I will show how to get to know them. There are some simple ways, that don't cost a lot of money, for us to become engrained in their lives like never before.

You've probably heard about positioning. It's the holy grail of marketing, a key step in creating the brand experience, and the main focal point of Chapter Eight. In this book, without a lot of fancy theory, I am going to show you how to create a positioning for your business that will help build the ultimate brand experience.

In Chapter Nine, I will go behind the curtain to one of the most fundamentally helpful tools in marketing. It's a classic from old school days, but I still use it almost every day. It will help put together all of the pieces that we've been building so far. It will help solidify the positioning for your small business.

In Chapter Ten, it's time we start reaching out to the customer. We'll take a look at the many ways we can intersect with their lives and give them the brand message. Here is where we introduce the concept of the touchpoint, another fundamental of the Experience Effect.

But just reaching the customer isn't enough; we have to choose the right time and the right place and string them all together. This is what I call a touchpoint tree. In Chapter Eleven I will show how to create one for your small business—it's a great way to visualize where the experiences will reach the customer.

The right place and the right time means nothing if we don't have the right message. In Chapter Twelve, I will show how to activate touchpoints by tailoring the brand message to make them appropriate to the medium. This is the crux of the Experience

Effect and it's crucial to getting customers engaged with the brand. It finally all comes together for a total brand experience.

We can't deny or ignore the digital revolution. In many ways, the digital world has made the brand experience so much more real and meaningful for customers. We'd be missing a huge piece of the Experience Effect if I didn't highlight the role of digital marketing in Chapter Thirteen. Besides, digital marketing is incredibly cost effective so we'll concentrate a lot of effort here.

In Chapter Fourteen, I talk about becoming a "benchmark brand"—an aspiration for all of us. We'll investigate what that means and how the Experience Effect can help a brand achieve benchmark status.

Really good marketing requires a long-term vision. Chapter Fifteen shows how to think beyond the daily crisis and how to manage the brand for the long run. We will work to get beyond the basic to-do list and short-term deadlines to a full-blown strategic plan—one that has a three-year horizon.

None of us act alone, and no matter how much of an entrepreneur we are, we have a team of people around us, helping us. We may not even realize it. In Chapter Sixteen, I hope to open your eyes to how motivating your team can help achieve success. We'll even dashboard it, a concept that I hope you find very useful.

And lastly, in Chapter Seventeen we will explore personal branding. When you run a small business, it's hard to separate yourself from the brand, and to a large degree you shouldn't. We'll talk about personal branding and the effect it can have on the business.

As we go through the process, I hope you will start thinking like a marketer, acting like a marketer, and being a brand. Perhaps this will be for the very first time, although I would wager you've been doing it all along without even realizing it. Now we can learn from the big boys just how to do it a little more methodically and successfully.

Enjoy building your Experience Effect every step of the way.

1 Marketing is Marketing
Lightly Starched

"Marketing is all about building a compelling brand experience for your customers that adds value to their lives."

Whether you realized it before or not, if you own a small business then you are also a marketer. Maybe you never trained to be one, but you are one now.

I'm not much for industry jargon and I certainly make it my business to avoid buzzwords, and I hate when people only talk in analogies. I laugh them off in fact.

I've been resisting the temptation, but I guess we need to start out with...a definition. All good business books do, right? I wouldn't want to disappoint the critics!

So let's begin Chapter One with a definition of marketing to start us out at the same place. First of all, please know that implicit in my definition of marketing is the word integrated. To me, all marketing is integrated—always has been and always will be.

I get a kick out of people who say that integrated marketing is the wave of the future. Since when was marketing ever not integrated? Maybe it's because I grew up on the client side of the business at Johnson & Johnson, and was always responsible for the entire brand, but to me marketing has always been integrated. The customer certainly sees it that way—one brand, one voice. The customer doesn't differentiate one form of messaging coming from the brand versus another.

With that off my chest, how do we define marketing? This should be easy textbook type stuff.

It's funny because one of the LinkedIn groups asked this very question of its members, "How would you define marketing?" At first, I thought it was the stupidest question I had ever heard. Everyone knows what marketing is, and everyone will define it the same way.

Then the definitions came rolling in—one after another, hour after hour, day after day. For months on end, members of that particular LinkedIn group sent in their own personal definitions of marketing. Some caused great debate, others immediate agreements.

I even threw in a comment or two because I found the whole exercise to be so much fun. I was surprised and intrigued, and here I am talking about it. This is exactly what our customers should be doing about our brands.

The LinkedIn exercise made me realize though that there really is no simple definition of marketing, and there is no one single answer. Everyone has a different take on it, which is why it's not a perfect science. There is just as much art to it as there is science.

How did I answer the question? My response shouldn't be so surprising given the titles of my books. Marketing is all about building a compelling brand experience for your customers that adds value to their lives.

Now if you've never been in marketing before, none of that will make sense. If you've already been doing marketing, then that sentence may be a new way of thinking about the craft. Either way, I hope that by the time you finish this book I will have you sold on the concept.

Think of your own behavior.

Like many people, I have a favorite dry cleaner that I go to all the time. They clean all of my shirts (and if you know me then you know I love my shirts), suits, pants...you name it. I go to this particular dry cleaner because they have never made a mistake, ever. They even catch things that I don't point out like stains or a loose hem—and they just fix them.

I don't even know what they charge me because I'm quite sure it's completely reasonable.

Now I've been to other dry cleaners in the neighborhood, several actually. And they all did a good job too. So why did I switch around until I found this particular one?

For one simple reason—at this dry cleaner, they remember me.

The employees/owners greet me on a first name basis, and say hello each time. They inquire about my kids and ask me if the clothes are coming out ok. The other places never really acknowledged me as a person. I would go into the store week after week, and they acted like they were seeing me for the first time.

I found it annoying, so I switched. The next dry cleaner I visited did the same thing, so I switched again.

I finally found a place that knew me by name, sort of like the bar Cheers. Now why was this so important to me? I actually had to stop and analyze my own behavior to figure it out. It's the emotional connection and the experience that made me finally stop looking for a "better" place.

For me, going to the same dry cleaner is a symbol of belonging to a community. Having the people there know me makes me feel like I'm a member of the neighborhood, and that people in the neighborhood really do know me and care about me on some level.

It's completely emotional. Again, the truth is that the other places did just as good a job of cleaning my clothes. There were no problems, but they didn't seem to care. What I haven't told you is that the place I go to regularly now is actually out of the way. I go out of my way to go there because it's a better experience. It is an experience that makes me feel better and that keeps me coming back.

Those emotions have turned what could easily be a generic dry cleaner into a...brand. It's the brand experience that has built my loyalty and keeps me coming back. It forced me to choose that brand over others of similar quality that were perhaps even a tad bit more convenient. A positive brand experience has the power to negate other factors.

Now that's good marketing. That's the Experience Effect!

Notice I didn't mention any advertising, and certainly no television advertising. You don't have to do advertising to do good marketing or to create a brand experience.

Chances are you don't own a dry cleaning business, and you probably don't run a Fortune 500 company, but that part doesn't matter. Marketing is marketing, big or small, regardless of the business. It's all about building an incredible experience for customers, whether you're cleaning their shirts or making them dinner or providing them with financial services.

The methodology needed to create an amazing brand experience remains the same whether you're Walmart, Coca-Cola, a local restaurant, a consultant, or Apple. It's the same marketing process regardless of the business. Sure, the budgets may be different, and the details work out differently, but how you get there is the same.

I believe that as a small business, you can in fact get the same kinds of results as the big brands, perhaps on a different scale, even without the big brand budgets. That's what this book is all about.

It takes a special kind of person to be an entrepreneur and to run a small business. It's not an easy life. It's not like small business owners are surrounded by lots of colleagues and a large support staff. Entrepreneurs do not have a clearly defined role within a well-oiled machine. None of us can count on others to watch our back or to cover us when we're out. There's no marketing team to do the heavy lifting for us.

Is that why we love it so much?

You may not have any formal marketing training—what you do know, you've learned along the way. With no MBA to fall back on, and no classic brand management training, you may just have a lot of experience and common sense, which quite honestly will do you well.

As a small business owner, you are now also a marketer, so add that to your resume. You are marketing your business—building a brand experience that will propel you to success.

This is marketing, defined. Welcome aboard.

2 Your Business is a Brand
Distinctive Stripes

"If you've got a product or service you want to sell, you must first turn it into a brand."

When asked the question,"What is a brand?" most people name something that they grew up with such as Tide, Crest, and Campbell's. Yup, check, those are brands.

I worked on quite a few big ones myself, including Kellogg's, Johnson's Baby, Arm & Hammer, and Nestle. These are big, huge blockbuster brands that we have incorporated into our lives, and as children, we often adopt these brands after watching our parents. We wash our clothes with them, brush our teeth with them, feed our tummies with them, and soothe our skin with them.

Many people think that a brand is a logo, a tagline, a package, or a website. While those are elements of a brand, there is a lot more in the making of a great brand experience.

Tide, Crest, Campbell's, and Johnson's Baby Products are not just ordinary detergents, toothpastes, food products, or personal care items. They are blockbuster brands, and we rely on them, know what to expect from them, and in most cases love them. Heck, we even "like" them on Facebook. With these brands come a promise and an expectation and that's what separates them from the other products in their categories.

We really could use any toothpaste product to brush our teeth—they all would work pretty well actually, but we choose Crest because of the emotional attachment we've made to that brand. It brings up childhood memories, feelings of security, and nostalgia for home. Think of the different emotions we all might have that come from using Crest toothpaste versus Arm & Hammer toothpaste. It totally depends on our personal perspective and personal experiences.

If you've got a product or service you want to sell, you must first turn it into a brand.

One of the great differences between a product and a brand is this emotional connection. It's one thing to need a product to get something done. We need to do our laundry, and we certainly need to eat every day, but when we choose a specific brand, we are doing so because we want to.

The "want" is the result of an emotional connection that has been created over time. That emotional connection turns a product into a brand.

We may need laundry detergent to do our laundry, but we choose Tide because we want that particular brand. It's often a very unconscious reason. Once the emotion of "want" enters the picture, a brand is created. Any product in a category can service the needs, but generally only one brand (or maybe two) can satisfy the wants.

Allow me to illustrate with a personal example. An example of where a need turns into a want, and a brand is born.

It's often said that a man is known for the company he keeps. Well, I'm known for the shirts I wear. Colorful, patterned shirts are a part of my "brand"—I wear a different one everyday. Do I need to wear a shirt? Absolutely, not too many clients would trust a marketing guy walking around the conference room without a shirt on. Plus, it gets kind of cold.

I need to wear a shirt, and it must be a shirt that is appropriate for work if I want to be taken seriously. There are certainly lots of products on the market that can fulfill that need. Banana Republic comes to mind almost by default (we'll get to that in Chapter Fourteen), and I am sure I could find plenty of choices at Sears and J.C. Penney.

However, I choose one particular brand, Paul Smith. I choose the Paul Smith brand because I want to wear Paul Smith shirts. It's a British fashion label that makes both men's and women's clothing. I can spot those stripes a mile away! I love Paul Smith—the brand has become a part of my identity.

I have other brands in my closet too, but honestly probably seventy-five percent of my shirts are from Paul Smith (and maybe a couple other brands). I want the Paul Smith brand.

You are probably wondering "Why does he want that particular brand? Maybe it's the distinctive stripes."

The bold colors and bright patterns make me feel like I'm unique and I'm not dressing like everyone else. The European cuts make me look just a little bit thinner, which isn't so bad. The classic designs don't go out of style, so my money is well invested.

I swear that I have gotten new business because of my shirts.

The shirts also make me feel like I'm just a little bit younger than I really am. In a very youth-oriented and youth-obsessed field like marketing and advertising, it's important to me to feel young. In a field that is packed with competition, many of which do a very good job, it's important to me to feel like I stand apart.

I love stopping in the store on 5th Avenue in New York. I've been there so many times that the sales associates all recognize me, even in the biggest city in the country. This location only features the men's line, so I get to browse around the entire store, not just one small section. The clothing is masterfully merchandised and organized to keep me moving from area to area. It's never fully crowded, so I can always try something on comfortably, even during the 40% off sale.

I "like" Paul Smith on Facebook, and I read the designer's blog posts. I even follow the brand on Twitter. I'm hopeless. I am not exclusive to Paul Smith, but I sure am loyal. Most days of the week I wear something from the brand, even if it's just a belt.

The truth is that I could wear any kind of shirt for work. Banana Republic would fit me fine and keep me warm. The same is true of Hugo Boss or Ralph Lauren.

I need clothes for work, but I want to wear Paul Smith.

It's because of the experience I have with the Paul Smith brand, every single time that keeps me coming back—it's because of the brand's marketing, the brand's Experience Effect.

The funny thing is that when I do wear a different kind of shirt, perhaps one less colorful or stylish, people comment! They ask me how I am feeling and will say, "Is everything ok? You don't seem like yourself today." The truth is, when I am wearing a different kind of shirt, I'm not myself. I'm not reflecting my brand.

Paul Smith has become a part of who I am.

I have immersed myself so deeply into the Paul Smith brand that my closet is filled with the brand's shoes, belts, pants, messenger bags, and cologne. I even own a Paul Smith collar and leash for my French bulldog Sophie! Paul Smith is a total experience for me. Now that's a brand, not just a shirt! We should aspire to get our customers thinking this way! For your small business, you certainly can do the same.

I'm sure you too can think of the many brands that you have incorporated into your life, because you want them there. Maybe it's a clothing brand or maybe a favorite brand of cereal. I'm sure there are many brands, now that I've got you thinking about it, that fill emotional needs in such a unique way that you wouldn't dream of choosing any other brand in that category. Kashi cereal is another one for me; my day just doesn't start out the right way without it.

Now translate that thinking to your business.

It's so vitally important to get to that emotional space with our customers too. Transcend being a product that people need, to something that they want because we add value to their lives. Get to a place where they can't live without the company. Connect with them on an emotional level, because then, and only then, will the business have become a brand.

Chapter 2: Your Business is a Brand

It may be hard at first, but I would bet that virtually every single business could have an emotional connection with its customers. Let's try to map out a few:

Small Business	Emotional Connection
Lawyer	Security
Doctor	Trust
Retail Store	Therapy (I like that one)
Cleaning Service	Indulgence
Consultant	Reassurance
Day Care	Nurture
Hair Salon	Attraction

Get the point?

The question is how to get there with your small business. At first, it may seem almost impossible to think of an emotional benefit to your brand, and some are certainly easier than others. To jumpstart the thought process, try focusing on the rational side first. Make a list of all the rational benefits that you provide for your customers. Think of everything that you do for them.

Now try to turn them into an emotional benefit. You may even be surprised that some of the items on your list are already an emotional benefit.

Here are a few examples from the big brands that may give us some help:

Brand	Rational Benefit	Emotional Benefit
Disney	Keep kids busy	Magic of childhood
Coca-Cola	Quench thirst	Be a part of America
Apple	Connect to the world	Look smart

I can tell you that the big brands spend a lot of time figuring out their emotional connections. They spend millions of dollars in research trying to crack the code on the emotional benefits of their brands—or at least the really successful ones do.

They listen to customers and they try to figure out what they really want. It's easy to determine their needs, not so easy to decipher their wants.

The key to determining the emotional connection of the brand is to really understand the customer. How they live their lives, what they need from you, and then ultimately what they want from you. We will explore how to target our customers and how to get to know them in Chapters Six and Seven.

A solid understanding of our customers will help lead us to figuring out the positioning of our business; something that we'll get to later in Chapters Eight and Nine.

All of this will get us on the path to turning the business into a brand. We have to create a brand in order to market it to our customers. In the end, the experience we build, based on an emotional connection, is what will make that happen.

It's time to build the experience, and thereby build the brand.

3 Creating the Experience Effect
The Super Brand

I've hopefully convinced you that you're a marketer and that your business is a brand—and that it's the emotional connection we create with our customers that makes us more connected to them than any other ordinary product or service.

This is what it means to be a brand.

Brands transcend the products themselves, and become much more meaningful to their customers than just the physical benefits.

Paul Smith is so much more than a shirt to me—it's a brand experience. My favorite neighborhood dry cleaner is so much more than just a place to get my shirts cleaned—it's also a brand experience different than any other.

The owner even included a hand-written thank you note with my shirts the other day. It really made my day.

It's the experience that I have with these brands that I want, that I count on, that I turn to over and over again. Creating this experience takes the brand to the next level—actually it takes the brand's relationship with customers to the next level. A consistently meaningful experience for customers is what builds loyalty and makes an impact on their lives—creating undeniable brand engagement. This, my friends, is the Experience Effect.

I can't think of a better way to define it.

The big brands certainly think about marketing this way, even if they don't call it the Experience Effect. They consciously map out the kind of interactions that they want their customers to experience at every moment with the brand, including the advertising, the website, Facebook, brochures, instore displays, etc.

Every moment is carefully planned to be consistent with the brand and with each other. Every moment is designed to impact their customers' lives, or at least that's the goal.

Let's look at an example that you may never have thought about before —the NFL (National Football League). On the surface the NFL may not seem like a brand, but it really is more than just an organization that aligns teams and players around the country. The NFL is an experience.

The basics of the NFL brand include the games we watch live in massive stadiums, or on television, and also all of the logo merchandise we buy as fans.

But there are also the websites, blogs, digital games, and social media that have become a huge part of experiencing professional football, beyond the real games themselves and the jerseys we buy online.

Hard-core fans can interact with the NFL every day on one device or another. They can play fantasy football and interact with other hard-core fans. They can analyze plays and speculate about the winners. Fans can learn about every morsel of a player's life and aspire to be just like him.

Then there's the Super Bowl—it's become a national holiday and has become engrained in pop culture. So much so, that many other brands now thrive on the activity. Have you ever visited a grocery store during the weeks leading up to the Super Bowl? The aisles are stocked with sales on alcohol and snack food, and it has become one of the biggest party occasions of the year. All of this is centered on the NFL and its competitive teams.

The Super Bowl is a brand in itself, complete with trademark protection.

In totality, the NFL brings families and friends together on a regular basis, even friends that don't really know each other. The NFL even advertises its brand experience, and encourages its fans to interact with the brand in multiple ways, motivating the behavior it is already witnessing with its biggest fans.

The NFL has an incredible Experience Effect.

Now on the flip side, take a look at Macy's. Once a dominant retail icon, I don't know what that brand is anymore. I know it's a department store, and it still plays a major role in the industry. I can buy stuff there, but why would I want to?

The brand is so incredibly inconsistent, it's mind-boggling—I don't know what it stands for. I have a feeling that it might stand for Americana (big huge star, Thanksgiving Day Parade, Fourth of July fireworks), but I'm just not sure.

Sure, there's the flagship store in New York, the world's largest single department store and a cool experience unto itself, but go to the Macy's at your local mall and it's a very different place. We're likely to see a cluttered, disjointed mess (at least in my opinion).

The advertising highlights wonderful collaborations with celebrity brands like Martha Stewart, Jessica Simpson, and Donald Trump, but when inside the stores it's very hard to navigate and find anything I want from these collaborations amidst all the clutter.

The stores on the West coast seem to be considerably nicer and more upscale than those on the East coast. I am not sure why the East coast and West coast stores are so different, so I find it very confusing. I can't tell what the Macy's brand is really all about. Although I do watch the Thanksgiving Day Parade every year as a tradition in my house, it never gets me to stop into a store because I know that I'm not going to like the experience there. The branding is far too in-consistent to engage me.

There's no Experience Effect at Macy's like there is at the NFL.

What is particularly troubling for the Macy's brand is all the competition it faces. There are so many options when it comes to de-partment store shopping. Macy's has strong competitors who know their brands very well and provide consistently effective shopping experiences for their specific target audienc-es.

Target and Nordstrom are two stellar examples. We know exactly what those brands are all about, and we get a very specific experience every time we visit any of their stores. Kohl's and Barney's are two other great department stores which offer great retail experiences, each in their own unique way for their customer base.

These are retail brands that have defined themselves in a very specific way, which is consistently reflected in the marketplace. These brands should offer good inspiration as we begin the process of building the Experience Effect for small businesses, particularly if you are in a retail business.

The examples noted above highlight, the good, the bad, and the ugly, in branding and creating a positive experience for your customers. Now here is a formal definition for the Experience Effect: when a brand consistently delivers a relevant and meaningful experience to its customers, it can have a profound effect on both the customers' lives and the business itself.

Take that to the bank!

4 Defining Your Brand
Give a Hoot

"When defining our brand, we should put as much clarity as possible into how the brand and the business are described."

Now is the time to get to the real work. In order to get started in the process of creating the brand experience, we have to very specifically describe what the brand is going to be all about. In the case of small business, it's even more important because with limited resources it's important to stay focused.

You may have never thought about it this way, but defining your business is a critical first step in developing the marketing plan.

We need a very well-crafted statement of the type of business we are in, and the type of customers we serve. We have to define what we stand for, and the types of products and services that our customers can expect from us. It truly is the first step in the process.

At first glance, defining the brand may seem very easy, but it actually takes some thinking, decision making, and maybe even some data gathering.

Take a lawyer as an example. It's pretty easy to define that brand—a person who practices law, right? But what kind of law, and for which kind of client? In what regions of the world? What style of law? Is the lawyer a hard-nosed bully or an empathetic counselor?

By answering some of these questions, how we define this brand of lawyer could go from "practices law" to "practices family law in the state of California by offering customized advice and a sympathetic ear for women who are dealing with family issues that require legal counsel and documentation."

Do you see how we can start to get a picture of what this brand of lawyer is all about? The second description was a lot more definitive than when we first started out with "practices law."

When defining our brand, we should put as much clarity as possible into how the brand and the business are described, so that we can start to build a brand experience to match.

Doctors shouldn't define their brand simply by "practicing medicine." Instead, specific kinds of doctors like dermatologists would potentially define their brand as "board certified aesthetic dermatologists, who specialize in non-invasive procedures that treat patients' skin to help them look their best."

An owner of a small retail store should not just say that the brand is "retail sales"—this is way too broad. Rather, the brand like a home store should be defined by stating, "offering local customers an assortment of home accessories that are procured from around the world to create an eclectic mix of must-have items to turn your house into a home."

This provides much better clarity about the kind of retail store it is, and the unique products it has to offer.

Now the truth is, that some of this language is getting into "positioning," which we will cover later in the book in Chapters Eight and Nine, but it's important at this early stage to get specific about the kind of business we are conducting. We won't worry about confusing positioning and brand definition at this point, because it doesn't really matter at the end of the day.

While it's important to be as specific as possible, we also want to be careful about not boxing the brand in too tightly and limiting our future opportunities.

For example, if a hair salon only defined itself as "women's hair cuts" then it would close itself out of new business building op-portunities with men, children, and even other salon services like hair color or mani-cures. The brand definition would perhaps be too limiting.

If it makes sense to be super specific, then that's fine, just do it consciously. I know of a salon in New York that specializes in only cutting women's curly hair. I know of another salon that specializes in just doing "blow outs." These are very specific brand definitions, but these salons have a big enough market to sustain a great business.

We have to be careful not to define the brand too tightly, though, which would close out business building opportunities. The lawyer we discussed, who practices family law in California for women, for example, is closing out opportunities to work with men (and in other states if he chose to become licensed outside of California) by being so specific.

The trick is to balance specificity and focus along with the ability to expand. When defining the brand, make sure to describe the type of business in a way that allows for growth over time. We need the ability to expand if we want the brand to continually grow.

Let's look at a few examples from the big brands.

If Tide simply thought of itself as a "washing machine cleaning detergent for customers" then it would only sell laundry detergent for use in the home. As a brand it could never expand into stain removers or fabric softeners or even commercial products. Tide-to-Go would have never happened.

Kellogg's has exhibited a wonderful ability to expand their products while still maintaining a degree of specificity. With Tony the Tiger as a popular brand icon, Kellogg's could have easily defined the Kellogg's brand as merely a "kids' breakfast cereal." Management kept the brand definition open though, so that Kellogg's Special K cereal could be created for adults focused on weight control and then they continued to expand to Kellogg's Special K breakfast bars (non-cereal) and even Kellogg's Special K crackers (for anytime snacking).

It might be fun to take a look at a few brands, and examine how they are defining their business, and what it might look like if the brand had been too restrictive.

Brand	Type of Business	Too Restrictive
Aleve	Family health	Pain relief
W Hotels	Hospitality	Business hotel
Sony	Entertainment	Music
Bic	Disposable consumer goods	Disposable pens
Apple	Personal electronics	Personal computers

The key is to balance going broad with being specific. Either way, try to be definitive so that the brand has proper meaning.

Now take a look at Ben & Jerry's. I think the brand probably defines itself as "super premium ice cream," and it has stayed very true to that definition through the years. It has not expanded beyond that definition other than in sizes and forms, and even then it has never introduced a half-gallon size because that would be inconsistent with its "super premium" status in the market. The focus has been on flavor development and unique combinations, like my personal favorite Chunky Monkey. It fits perfectly!

The key is to know who you are as a brand and then to define it well—and be consistent (we'll get to that later). We will use this brand definition to guide the entire process of building the Experience Effect for your small business. It will help us to offer products and services to customers, and even decide which customers are best suited for the brand. It will help us create the right kind of experience to offer them so that it's relevant to them.

The brand definition will basically guide our major moves as a marketer.

None of this is easy, though. As a starting point, I find it useful to pick a few words to use to quickly describe the business. Single words or phrases that basically highlight what the brand offers to customers tend to work best. Start very factual and then grow from there.

Let's say that you are a tax consultant for individuals. You could use these three phrases to begin to describe the brand:

- Knowledge of government regulations

- Preparation of tax returns

- Advice on money management

The brand definition is starting to take some shape for this tax consultant. The phrases help describe the consultant as a very informed, useful resource for people who need help filing their taxes and maintaining their financial affairs.

Keep the brand definition going by adding in three more phases that now show more emotional benefits:

- Turn-key process with no hassle

- Unique ways to organize and reduce stress

- Techniques to maximize refunds and savings

By adding in a few emotional dimensions, we are contributing greatly to the brand definition. We can literally start to see and even picture this tax consultant's business and the kinds of services offered. You want to get to that point with your small business brand.

Complete the same exercise by coming up with three factual statements about your business as well as three emotional ones. You'll have the beginning of a very well defined brand and ultimately a powerful brand experience.

Write these statements either as the brand exists today or as you aspire it to be—or maybe even a mix of both. The brand definition should give direction for the future as well as for today. These descriptors will also give you a head start to creating a positioning statement for the brand, something we'll tackle in Chapters Eight and Nine.

If done well, the brand definition will help make sure that we stay true to the brand and that we behave consistently each and every time, which is a key tenant to the Experience Effect.

Again, don't get too tightly defined. We want to keep our options open for business growth. We will need to give the brand definition room to evolve over the years, as the marketplace changes. New technologies, new competition, new attitudes and behaviors are all factors we will want to consider as we keep an eye on how we define the brand. We will want to capitalize on new opportunities as they arise, even if it means evolving the brand definition, just a little at a time.

We also want to keep the brand definition fresh. A brand that stays stagnant loses its relevance eventually.

Let's take a look at the adult-themed restaurant chain Hooters. Hooters was a well-defined brand (at least at the start) that was incredibly successful in the beginning as a fun "adult" restaurant to hang out with friends. Lots of brand experience here, shall we say! Not a place for a date, that's for sure. But through the years, as the restaurant industry evolved and new concepts took shape.

Hooters remained too much the same.

Now in some circumstances, that might be ok, but in the case of Hooters, the brand lost its uniqueness. It lost its sizzle in a marketplace that is always dynamically changing. The brand got old and should have evolved with the times, to stay relevant to customers who are looking for dining and entertainment experiences.

Don't let this happen to your small business. Define it well, but keep it flexible enough to evolve over time to capitalize on marketplace opportunities, and changing tastes and preferences.

Now take a look at HGTV, a brand defined around advice and resources to improve your home. It includes television shows, internet content, brand collaborations in products and services—who knows what's next.

All of the brand experiences are emerging and growing out of a simple, but flexible brand definition—making a profound effect on those of us that are into home improvement, in the type of channel we prefer to experience.

This leaves me with just one question for you: what kind of business are you in?

Chapter

5 Tracking Your Competition
Circling Main Street

"The point is that we should open up our minds to a broader competitive set—to players that are beyond the close-in competitors."

Now that we have the brand defined, it's important to measure it against the competition. If you are running a business, any kind of business, you are probably keenly aware of the competitors. You probably know their offerings, their pricing, and their competitive advantages.

If you don't, then consider this a kick in the pants.

On virtually every marketing team I have ever participated in, there was always at least one person who was responsible for tracking the competition. It was their job to gather all the competitive information on a regular basis, usually monthly, and then distribute it to the rest of the team.

While all of the team members might help gather information from their perspective on the business, everyone would funnel it to one point person who would organize it and make sense of it.

Through great team effort, the big brands track every aspect of their competitors' marketing activity, including, but not limited to:

* Advertising spending in television, print, newspaper, local, radio, billboard, transit, online, etc.

* Couponing, both online and offline. Online couponing has become very influential in driving traffic to local businesses. It's vitally important to track this activity among your competitors.

* Promotional activity, including sweepstakes and contests.

* Social marketing as played out on sites like Facebook, Twitter, Foursquare, and LinkedIn.

* Websites (be on the lookout for multiple micro-sites that may come from the same brand).

* Packaging and package inserts.

Take a lesson here and create a similar list of activity to track for your competitors. Make it someone's job to track all of the competitors' activity. Have someone compile a monthly report of all the relevant activity. Dedicate someone to "like" Facebook pages of other brands and follow Twitter streams.

Even if that someone is you!

It's not easy and it takes commitment. In some ways, the big brands do have it a lot easier since they can hire services to do the tracking and the compiling. Technology exists in many categories to do the heavy lifting.

Small businesses generally do not have that luxury, but there are still many ways to track competition without spending a lot of money and taking up all of your time.

What are some of the most obvious ways to track the competition? Google alerts—they are free, and couldn't be easier to set up. If you don't have Google alerts set up for your main competitors, and for your own brand too, then do it right now.

It takes a mere few minutes right from the Google homepage. Here are some other easy things you can do to get a handle on what the competition is doing:

- "Like" and "Follow" your competition on Facebook and Twitter (make sure you track both the brand name as well as the owners or key leaders—it's all very insightful).

- Enroll in email marketing campaigns and CRM (consumer relationship marketing) programs.

- Conduct secret shopping trips to participate in the retail experience.

- Order competitive products to see what the process is like and what comes along with the packaging.

- Go to trade shows, visit the relevant booths, and pick up the collateral material.

- Visit the websites and devour every word that is written, and try to uncover how competitors are presenting their brands.

The key is to not just track them, but learn from them. Analyze each experience to determine the pros and the cons. What's working for the competition and what is not? Replicate the marketing tools that seem to be working in your competition's favor, and determine the best and most effective ways to reach your customers.

Make sure that all the marketing elements that form your brand experience are even better than those of the competitors.

If a Facebook page impresses you, then use it as inspiration for your own Facebook page. If you find one of your competitor's customer service representatives is really helpful, then apply what you liked about what they did to your business. If you are fascinated by a certain claim, then try to understand why and how it could apply to your brand.

It's not "stealing," it's learning and reapplying.

This knowledge will also help to define the brand as we discussed in Chapter Four. What competitive businesses should we be following? Don't stay too narrowly focused.

It is very easy to identify close-in competition—those other brands that offer exactly what we do. If you are a tax consultant, then it's easy to identify the other tax consultants in the same area. If you own a woman's clothing store, then it's easy to figure out other women's clothing stores in the area or the Starbucks up the street if you operate a coffee shop or breakfast diner.

This is of course a good place to start, no doubt about that. These close-in competitors are the players that you are fighting against day-in and day-out. Yet, by looking beyond the obvious we can learn so much more and perhaps stay even more in tune to what is happening in the marketplace.

I want you to think about the actual competition much more broadly, because that is what the big brands do.

Take Diet Coke as an example. Sure, Diet Pepsi is the closest competitor—most can barely tell the difference (well I can, but that's not something to be proud of!). Diet Pepsi and the other caffeinated diet sodas are the closest competitors to Diet Coke and the brand methodically tracks every move that these competitors make, but the competition isn't limited to just those other few brands.

Diet Coke competes against other no-calorie drinks as well, like Vitamin Water Zero and Diet Snapple. It also competes against no-calorie drink mixes like Crystal Light and Kool-Aid. Diet Coke certainly competes against bottled water, even though there's no caffeine, and clearly it competes against other caffeinated drinks like coffee and tea.

No go even broader. Think about stopping into a convenience store to pick up a drink. We've got two bucks in our hand and we are about to buy a Diet Coke. On the way to the refrigerator section, we pass so many choices for how to spend those two dollars. Snack food, baked goods, even something to read.

At that moment, in that venue, all of those things are competitors to a Diet Coke purchase.

We could go crazy here and get so lost that we never track anything, but don't get carried away. The point is that we should open up our minds to a broader competitive set, as they say, to players that are beyond the close-in competitors.

We must even consider things completely outside of the business that still compete for our customers' attention.

If you operate a small retail women's clothing store on Main Street, you should certainly consider the other small retail stores on the same street as competitors, and also the clothing stores in other parts of town and at the mall.

Do not just view the other small stores in your town as your competition, but also the big stores too!

If you don't also consider online clothing retailers to be your competition, then this is a serious oversight. It's been said that online sales have had the most impact on small businesses. It's hard to compete with the prices and the convenience of ordering from home.

As a small retail storeowner, the competition is much broader than what we've just listed. You are competing for customers' cash, so the competition is all local businesses that are fighting for that customers' business. Hair salons, restaurants, entertainment, you name it. If a portion of the business is from gift giving, there are a lot of choices for people to give gifts—even movie gift certificates or flowers for that matter.

If you are a business consultant, you've got competition too—from other business consultants for sure, but also from internal resources, larger agencies, and even just "nothing." The customer could easily just cancel the project. Think broadly about the brand's competition so that you know what you are up against in the marketplace.

I find it useful to build concentric circles to help visualize the competition across the board. Concentric circles look like this:

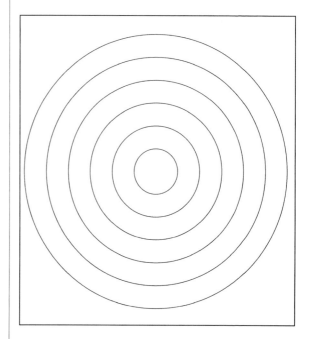

The inner circle, or core, is where we put the brand. Each ring represents another layer of competition. The closer to the type of business we are in, then the closer the concentric circle is to the core. Here's an example for Diet Coke that we just outlined:

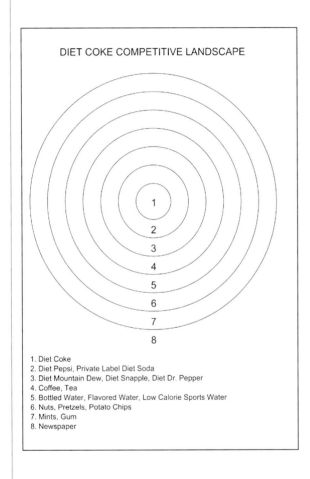

DIET COKE COMPETITIVE LANDSCAPE

1. Diet Coke
2. Diet Pepsi, Private Label Diet Soda
3. Diet Mountain Dew, Diet Snapple, Diet Dr. Pepper
4. Coffee, Tea
5. Bottled Water, Flavored Water, Low Calorie Sports Water
6. Nuts, Pretzels, Potato Chips
7. Mints, Gum
8. Newspaper

Notice how having a visual helps make it all so much easier to understand. Also, notice how I plotted the competition based on being in a convenience store. For a brand like Diet Coke, the competition varies on the venue and the usage occasions.

Big bottles of Diet Coke in a supermarket have different competition than single serving cans in a convenience store. We won't go crazy here, though. We'll just stick to the convenience store, single serving part of the business for illustration purposes.

Can you see how having this kind of outlook on the competition can provide new direction for thinking about the business? Now, let's do the same exercise for the retail clothing store on Main Street:

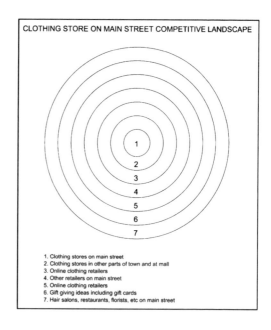

CLOTHING STORE ON MAIN STREET COMPETITIVE LANDSCAPE

1
2
3
4
5
6
7

1. Clothing stores on main street
2. Clothing stores in other parts of town and at mall
3. Online clothing retailers
4. Other retailers on main street
5. Online clothing retailers
6. Gift giving ideas including gift cards
7. Hair salons, restaurants, florists, etc on main street

This graphic depiction of the competition will help in so many ways to:

- Define the brand even further since you'll see how distinctive you need to be in the marketplace.

- Identify the real competition, those both near and far out, much more clearly.

- Prioritize competitive threats—certainly activities from those closer to the core are going to pose a greater risk to the business.

- Craft a brand experience that is unlike anything else on those concentric circles.

I often find that I learn more from the competition that is in the outer rings than from my competitors in the inner rings. I already understand the close-in competitors, it's the ones far out that I can learn the most from because they could be more of a competitive threat than I originally thought.

In business-to-business industries (B2B), I believe that "nothing" is a far bigger competitive threat than other business consultants in the same industry. In my opinion, the fact that the client may cancel the project without warning, at any time, poses the biggest threat.

Knowing which threats are most significant will help you form a very different defensive strategy to deal with your "competition"—and may require a much more proactive approach than you had otherwise thought would be necessary.

Food for thought—what's in your circles?

6 Identifying Your Customer
You're Family

"By using both demographic and psychographic information, we can more accurately describe our target customer and put better definition around it."

If we've ever worked together, then you know I believe that marketing begins and ends with the customer—specifically with your target customer. Every step we take in marketing the brand should be done in consideration of the customer and what they need and what they want.

Let the customer be our guide.

Think about the decisions we face over the course of a year in business. Every decision should be carefully weighed and carefully considered based on how the customer will react. Keep the customer in mind on every aspect of the brand, including:

- Pricing

- Product offerings

- Company hours

- Marketing campaigns

- Website developments

- Social media commentary

- Customer service (obviously)

This notion of taking customers into consideration is something that was drilled into my head in graduate school at Columbia, and again during my time in marketing at Johnson & Johnson. I took several consumer behavior classes that all focused on understanding and acknowledging the customer.

If we are not thinking about the customer all day long, then we are not going to be able to market to them very well.

In order to think about the customer, we need to know who they are. Similar to the manner in which we defined our brand in Chapter Four, we also need to define who we want our customer to be.

Who is the ideal customer for the business? Who will the offerings appeal to the most? For whom is the brand best suited?

Marketers call this process targeting. You've probably heard the phrase "target market" a lot. A target market is basically the type of customer who is most appropriate for the brand. The target market is our best chance at appealing to someone—someone specific.

The reason it's called "target" is because it should be specific, and the more specific the better.

So where do we start? One place is the brand definition. By creating the specific brand definition as we did in Chapter Four, we should be able to use it to start to define the customer.

Start by listing out the common attributes of your customers. Are most of them women? Do they tend to fall in a certain age range? What part of the country do they live? Do they have any common characteristics?

Start to compile any of the facts that could be used to describe the average, most likely customer for the business.

We can also do a survey, either in person or online, to ask customers some questions. We can politely interrupt our customers and ask them about themselves. Most are pretty happy to share, as social media has certainly taught us.

We can ask easy multiple-choice questions but also include some open-ended ones as well. Queries like "What is most important to you?" or "What's your greatest fear?" It will be eye opening to see if there are any commonalities across the survey respondents.

If your business has a Facebook page, this is a great spot to do a little survey. A major benefit of using Facebook for surveys is that the social media platform can give analytics on all of the "likes." This will paint a nice picture of who is visiting and commenting on the posts you create. You'll literally get to see "who likes" your brand.

If there is no Facebook page, then we can always use email addresses that we've captured or online services like SurveyMonkey. If there are no email addresses, then start collecting them ASAP. You'll be able to use them for quite a few purposes, just make sure to ask people permission and to "opt in" for further communication.

It is incredibly important to be as specific as possible about the target market. The more specific you are, the more likely you'll be able to create a compelling brand experience for your customers.

For example, to say that customers are women is not specific enough for targeting and for building a brand experience. We would want to get much more detailed about the kind of women to target, the kind of women that would want our brand.

We'll want to know if she is a younger woman, say 21–34 years old. Is she married with children? Higher income? Does she own a home?

That's a little bit more specific, although we can do better.

These little tidbits are all demographics—facts and figures about the target audience. Demographics start to give us a picture of the target market from a factual standpoint but we do need more. Demographics are very rational aspects of who we would want to be our customer, but we want some emotional aspects as well.

We can even further define our target market by adding in psychographics.

While demographics are facts and figures that describe a group's physical properties, psychographics describe a group's attitudes and behaviors, such as how the group feels and acts.

Where does she like to shop? What does she do on a Friday night? How does she feel about the current state of the economy? What is she afraid of? These are all psychographic questions that add dimension to the target market.

I would add open-ended questions into the survey, because answers to these types of questions make the targeting much richer and give us a definitive glimpse into a target customer's life.

By using both demographic and psychographic information, we can more accurately describe our target customer with much better depth. We can start to more specifically build a certain kind of brand experience that the target customer will like.

I would encourage picking just one target market and owning it. Focus on it and make them fall in love with the brand over and over. We can have more than one for sure, but let the budget and resources make that decision. If you can afford to go after more than one target market, then it is certainly a good way to grow the business.

Don't pick target markets that are diametrically opposed to each other, though, because it will be hard to appeal to different customers who are vastly different from each other.

Here is one example. It would be hard to market a business consultancy service for companies that are big and small, domestic and global, and in industries far and wide. However, a business consultancy that targets industries and companies that are adjacent to each other could possibly work—like companies in the food industry and in the restaurant industry.

The real point here, though, is that we can't be everything to everybody. Trying to target all customers will result in a brand which appeals to no one. Be specific about which target market to go after and find a rich business opportunity that will be successful with that particular market.

Do not create a brand that tries to be all things to all people, because this will leave you exhausted and unsuccessful.

Trying to be all things to all people may be the root of the problem with Macy's department store as we discussed in Chapter Three. The brand is not well targeted, and as a result it appears to be a mixed bag of mer-chandise and benefits without any clear focus.

Picking one core target market based on de-mographic and psychographic information can lead to very successful branding.

Let's take a look at some successful big brands and whom they may be targeting:

Brand	Demographic	Psychographic
Victoria Secret	Young women	Believe lingerie is fashion
Gillette	Adult men	Concerned with grooming
Burton	Teenage boys	Serious about the snow
Barack Obama	Young voters	Frustrated with status quo

Obviously these brands have much more in-formation to define their targets, and in fact I may not even have any of it right.

My point, though, is that the psychographics can help add dimension to the demographic information, so take note of how I added both dimensions into the targets.

As we start to compile these little facts and figures, list them out on a chart to have them in one place. On the left side column, list the demographic information and on the right side column list the psychographic information. Make sure both columns are long and full of information, because we'll need both sides to have a full picture. This list will come in handy later.

We will now have a nicely defined target market for the brand, a clear picture of who the most likely customer is for the business. It's a critical step in building the Experience Effect.

The Olive Garden certainly knows targeting well; I am quite impressed. The very successful restaurant chain has a very clearly defined customer for its offerings: middle-income families with multiple children, living in the suburbs, who long to spend more quality time together.

Olive Garden is the place that families gather to sit around the table, break some bread, share some pasta, and catch up.

We can see this targeting very clearly in the marketing, and clearly Olive Garden has built their brand experience to cater to this very specific customer. It's not for date night, and it's not a teen scene. It's for families.

"When you're here, you're family," as the brand states in its tagline.

The food is specifically designed for families to share and is moderately priced to not break the bank for a party of four or five with family style pasta-based dishes. The advertising nails it, but then all the other marketing elements come together as well to provide a total family dining experience. Everything that the brand communicates is directed toward families. It's excellent targeting that then generates excellent marketing.

If you own a restaurant, take note of this targeted marketing approach and try to replicate it to fit your intended audience. Who is your specific customer? Families, couples on a date, teens, or singles?

Knowing your customer will guide the kind of brand experience to create for them.

This is true not just for restaurants, but also for any small business. Defining the target market is a key ingredient in the success of marketing one's business.

Now that we've picked our target market, we need to get to know them.

Chapter

7 Getting To Know Your Customer
Hang It Up

"Data is only as good as the action we take with it. So make it all real and actionable."

Now that we've identified our target market, and our ideal customer, we now need to get to know them. We need to understand how they live their lives and how they go about their days—what their needs are and what they want out of life.

Part of being a marketer is becoming an expert on the lives of our customers. It's the only way we can possibly build a brand experience for them that will add value to their lives.

The big brands have entire teams dedicated to consumer research. This research may include tracking behaviors and attitudes, measuring response rates, and analyzing trend reports. These large corporate brands utilize a mix of methodologies to keep pace with consumers, and they hire outside resources to help their internal staffs stay on top of consumer learning.

These large brand names mix third party syndicated research data (information you can buy that already exists) with proprietary studies (information you gather on your own that's just about your brand) to get a full picture. They conduct qualitative research (small numbers of research participants) along with quantitative research (large numbers of research participants to be statistically significant) to test hypotheses and to then substantiate them.

They make consumer learning an ongoing effort every day of the year.

As a small business, you probably don't have those resources at your disposal, yet you still need some of that information to get to know your customers. You may not even understand anything in that last paragraph.

That's ok, you don't really need to!

The truth is that we can probably replicate a lot of the learning in a much more cost-effective manner for small business. We actually may not need full research reports and data analytics. We just need to do a few smart things, continually, and we'll have enough to keep our own consumer knowledge active and up-to-date.

A well-defined target market, like we discussed in Chapter Six, will also make getting to know our customers a lot easier. Focus is the key to efficiency here. A few clever tactics to learn about customers will keep research costs contained within a limited budget. Some things won't cost anything at all, while others may require a minor amount of spending.

Once you've identified the target customer, find out if you personally know anyone who fits the profile. You probably have friends and family members who could be a great place to start. Interview them and get to know them. Follow them for a day and see how they live their lives, manage their struggles, and fulfill their needs. Walk in their shoes for a day and see what it's like. Ask them if they have friends who would be willing to let you do the same.

When researching friends and family to learn more about your target customers, remember that it doesn't matter if they are actually your customers or not, in fact it would be nice to get a mix of customers and non-customers. See what the differences are between people who have bought into the brand versus those who have not done so yet. Take lots of notes and lots of pictures—they will come in handy later.

It will make the time more effective and "shareable" with the rest of the team.

Consider asking some of your current customers if they would mind being interviewed. You will find that many people would love to help out and to share their thoughts to help make your brand stronger. It is just as refreshing for them to express themselves, as it is for you to hear their thoughts.

Quick informal surveys among current customers are a great way to get to know them, without troubling them too much. Collect their names and send them emails or even give them a paper survey to fill out. We talked about this in Chapter Six when we were defining the target market, but really getting to know customers requires a much deeper approach. A deeper, more detailed survey could therefore help add more content to your understanding.

There are other things we can do too.

Watch the television shows that customers watch, read the magazines they read, go to the movies that they like. Following pop culture trends that influence customers is a great way to get to know the day-to-day things that they value in their lives like entertainment, food, family, and activities.

I was once doing a presentation for a fashion retailer that was targeting young women who are in the very early stages of their careers. The brand offers age-appropriate professional clothing for the young career woman. I didn't really know much about this segment, so I had to do some learning. The client supplied us with some market research decks, but quite honestly it all felt like a bunch of facts and figures. I couldn't get a real sense of these women, and had to do a little bit of my own research.

I asked a couple friends who had nieces this age if I could speak with them. I went shopping with these young women, took a look at their resumes, and listened to the struggles they were facing as they were starting their careers.

By meeting with these women, I discovered that although fashion may seem like a frivolous thing to some, it is actually quite important to this target customer, and ironically a source of real stress. These women didn't know how to dress for work and didn't really know what was appropriate for their age and stage of career. The notion of business casual was quite intimidating to these young career women.

I truly tried to step into the shoes of this target customer by reading some of their favorite magazines and visiting several of the websites that they frequent on a regular basis. In doing so, I started to get a very clear picture of who this woman was and how the brand could help her.

The learning process started to create a picture of how the brand could build an experience for her that would help to address her fashion needs at work and more importantly, reduce her stress about buying the right clothing.

This knowledge was power, and quite honestly, it was more helpful than the reams of data from the client. It didn't cost me a dime, really (other than a couple magazines, some movie tickets, and some coffee here and there).

Now, we clearly have to be careful about making broad generalizations about consumer behavior based on a few interviews and websites, but this kind of grassroots research can certainly add dimension to the data we may already have, and it can certainly start to fill in the holes where we have no data.

Consumer learning is all about texture and at the very least, this kind of grassroots research can certainly provide texture.

Similar to my advice in Chapter Five regarding tracking your competition, you should also make it someone's job to track consumer behavior as well. Perhaps this will even be your job—there's really nothing more important to the brand. Document everything so that you can create an amazing reference tool for the team.

Keep up on this research, since it's important to track how consumer behaviors change over time and as they progress through their lives.

It's important to get to know customers better than the competition does. We'll want to build a deeper bond with them to build brand loyalty. In fact, the competition is also a great source for learning as well. Paying attention to what they do, what they say, and how they say it gives a great view into how they think about the customer.

Learn from their efforts.

At the end of the day, what we want to do is to turn all of this learning into real action. I can tell you that this is where a lot of the big brands fall down. They have so much data that they don't know what to do with it, and they sometimes fall into the trap of never doing anything with it at all.

Data is only as good as the action we take with it, so make it all real and actionable.

Many of the big brands write out consumer profiles to use as a reference. I teach a marketing class at New York University (NYU), and we spend a lot of time on consumer profiles. It's the pivotal homework assignment that each student writes between the two very intense all day sessions.

The consumer profile takes all of the learning we've gained about the customer, and puts it into a tangible and real account of their life as it relates to the brand. It takes the factual data as well as the emotional, and weaves it into a story. It brings the customer to life.

Consumer profiles are written in prose, and tell a story about the life that the consumer lives. While they are very effective, I'd actually like to see something more visual and perhaps even more actionable for use in your small business.

Instead of creating a consumer profile, let's build a collage about the customer. While doing the consumer research we've been talking about (following and interviewing customers), take lots of pictures of them in action. While reading one of the magazines they read, tear out some key visuals. Cut out words that could describe the customer. Basically assemble a bunch of visuals that capture the essence of the customer, and put them into a collage.

It will become a fun, visual depiction of the customer that you can hang up in the office and that can serve as a constant reminder of why you are in business.

Building a collage can also be a great team exercise. Have each key staff member build a customer collage of their own and have them share with each other. Compare and contrast them, and use them as learning tools to get to know the customer as best you can.

If you've got more than one target customer, than do more than one collage. You can even do a few collages for the same customer, just to show the many dimensions. By doing a few customer collages, we add texture to the data, and make it a lot easier to make marketing decisions about how to reach and connect with our customers.

The point of the exercise here is to have the customer constantly in mind. Not an hour should go by that our customers' needs don't come into consideration, regardless of the business decision.

Keeping the customer at the forefront of your decision making is what marketing, both big and small, is all about, and having a customer collage will help to remind you of this fact.

8 Positioning Your Brand
You're In Good Hands

> *"Positioning is the mental space that we want to occupy in the customer's mind."*

It's time to put the brand definition and customer understanding together into what is probably the most confusing aspect of marketing—positioning. Many people have very divergent interpretations of what positioning is, which on the one hand is ok. But on the other hand, it can lead to a lot of very unproductive conversations and misinterpretations.

To tell you the truth, I find that most marketing people don't really know what positioning is.

Positioning is not a claim, and it's not a promise. It's not really a tagline either, although the tagline is the nearest thing in the marketplace to capturing it.

Despite its inherent confusion, positioning is potentially the most important aspect of building the brand experience. It's kind of like the summation of everything we've been exploring so far: brand definition, target market, competitive assessment, etc., and, as we've been saying, it starts with a really good understanding of the customer.

So now that you are a marketer, and you're turning your small business into a brand, let's get this mystery of marketing right. Let's start out with what positioning really is. If you can understand this, then you are truly, officially a marketer.

Scratch that, truly, officially a really good marketer!

To prove my point, I asked visitors to my website (JimJosephExp.com) to give me their definition of "positioning" on my message board there. Hoping to only get really one answer, I hit "enter" on the keyboard as I posed the question.

What type of answers did I receive when I asked for a definition of "positioning?"

One person responded with this definition, "It is the process of creating a unique image of your brand in your customer's mind that is different from competitor's products."[1] I like this definition because it is very visual; it's always easier to understand something when you put a picture to it.

---

1. Comments from "What is Your Definition of Positioning?" no longer available. The Experience Effect, accessed August 18, 2011, http://jimjosephexp.squarespace.com/.

Another respondent said this about positioning, "It is the process of a brand creating an emotional position in a customer's mind. So when a customer thinks of a brand it gives them that 'feeling' so it knows what to expect and wants to expect. Hence, a customer is attracted to that brand just for that reason—to fulfill that emotional expectation."[2]

See how confusing this can all be?

And yet another person defined positioning this way, "Finding the right price point and unique value proposition for your brand. Positioning can also fill a void in the marketplace and sometimes correlates with the research results of user centered design."[3]

See how quickly it can get so complicated, and become filled with mumbo jumbo? I hate buzzwords in marketing; I think they confuse the point even further.

Positioning is one of those nebulous concepts that is kind of hard to pin down—yet at the same time, it is so important to the success of the brand. It is at the heart of what the brand is all about,

---

2. Comments from "What is Your Definition of Positioning?" no longer available. The Experience Effect, accessed August 18, 2011, http://jimjosephexp.squarespace.com/.
3. Comments from "What is Your Definition of Positioning?" no longer available. The Experience Effect, accessed August 18, 2011, http://jimjosephexp.squarespace.com/.

because it encapsulates everything known and understood about the customer, and everything developed for the business.

I want clarity, so I want to simplify all of this so that you can actually apply it to your business. Positioning is not a buzzword, and it's not marketing du jour. It's a fundamental aspect of the process of marketing, and honestly we can't have a business plan without it, so it's important to really understand what it is.

Positioning starts with the brand definition but goes so much further.

Here's how I generally define it, in its most simple form: positioning is the mental space that we want to occupy in the customer's mind about the brand. It's how we want our customers to picture the brand, and it's the first thing that we want people to think about when they hear the brand name.

Positioning is essentially the emotion we want our customers to feel about our brand. It's how we want our brand "positioned" in their minds.

Can you see that positioning should be inherently emotional?

In Chapter Two, we discussed how an emotional connection with customers is the key to being a brand. That emotional bond should be reflected in the positioning statement for the business. Positioning is more about emotion, and less about the facts.

This is why when marketers think that a claim is a positioning statement, they are really missing the boat.

Once it's nailed, the positioning then becomes the basis for the brand experience. The key is to make sure that the actual brand experience delivers on what was intended in the positioning.

We'll get to that all in due time.

Let's take a look at what some of the big brands do for their positioning. Hint: you can often determine a brand's positioning by looking at its tagline.

Brand	Tagline
BMW	The Ultimate Driving Machine
All State	You're in Good Hands
L'Oreal	You're Worth It
Crest	Healthy, Beautiful Smiles for Life

One of my favorites is "Like a Good Neighbor, State Farm is There." Now that is positioning.

When creating a brand positioning, you will find that you can't please everybody all of the time. There is a lot of conversation on social media outlets about how this tagline makes no sense anymore. Many say that they don't know their neighbors. Is this a sign of the times, and the need for State Farm to adjust to changing norms or is this just really good targeting?

Notice the level of emotion in each of those taglines, which gives us a hint at their full positioning:

Brand	Positioning
BMW	Makes me feel powerful
All State	Provides safety, security
L'Oreal	Gives me self-esteem
Crest	Looking good for life

From State Farm's tagline we can interpret the positioning to be, "Someone I trust who is there when I need them."

These are all incredible taglines, built around emotion, that give us a hint at the brand's positioning. These brands very clearly tell us how they want us to think about them and how they want us to feel.

You can do the same with your small business.

There's something else to consider here—the competition. Part of the magic of positioning is that it needs to be unique. Your brand and only your brand should have your distinct positioning in the marketplace.

If everyone is doing their job well, then no two brands will be alike.

Notice how the two insurance companies, State Farm and All State, both have positioning unique to each other, yet they both offer the same rational benefit. They both could make the same claims, but they offer different emotional benefits.

To make sure that we are unique to the competition, we have to do some more homework, and check out the emotional benefits and positioning that the competition is using.

We'll want to make sure that our work is unique.

I use a simple little tool to help visualize a brand's positioning versus its competition. I like visuals, because they can bring clarity to a situation and also help with the decision-making process.

It's simply a positioning spectrum.

A horizontal line that shows the range of positioning and emotional benefits for a given category, with the various competing brands plotted along the line. On one end of the spectrum are the purely functional benefits of the category, and on the other end are the purely emotional benefits of the category, drawn like this:

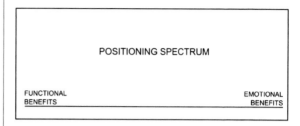

So to the left, we put brands that have a completely functional positioning or communications platform to their target market, and to the right, we put brands that have a completely emotional positioning or communications platform to their target audience. All of the other brands that have a combination of functional and emotional positioning fall somewhere in between. The more emotionally based a brand is, the further to the right it shall be placed on the spectrum, like this:

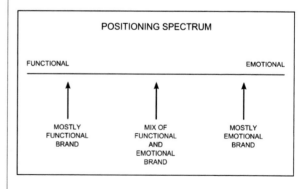

By plotting brands onto this spectrum, we can see the range of communications that customers are absorbing in any given category, and how distinctive each brand is from each other. We can also tell which brands have a more emotional story than others.

The key for us is to make sure that our positioning is not only emotionally based, but also distinctive from the competition. Our positioning should also be relevant to our customers, but if we know them well, we should have already taken care of that.

It's important to plot the brands in the category, and to include a snapshot of their positioning, perhaps by using their taglines.

Let's try an example, using insurance companies.

Insurance brands are an interesting example since there is so much functionality to insurance when it comes to coverage, quotes, and mechanics. There's also a huge emotional side when it comes to protecting your family and livelihood. In this industry, there are a lot of brands with very similar offerings, and it may be hard to tell one apart from the other. Or is it?

Here's how a positioning spectrum might lay
out for the brands:

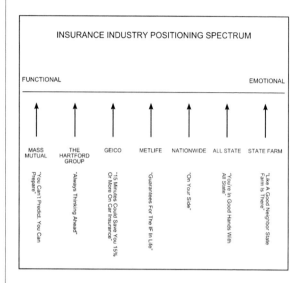

INSURANCE INDUSTRY POSITIONING SPECTRUM

FUNCTIONAL   EMOTIONAL

MASS MUTUAL	THE HARTFORD GROUP	GEICO	METLIFE	NATIONWIDE	ALL STATE	STATE FARM
"You Can't Predict, You Can Prepare"	"Always Thinking Ahead"	"15 Minutes Could Save You 15% Or More On Car Insurance"	"Guarantees For The IF In Life"	"On Your Side"	"You're In Good Hands With All State"	"Like A Good Neighbor State Farm Is There"

I bet at first thought you imagined that all
those brands would be in the same spot,
right?

By using a positioning spectrum, we see
how the different brands prioritize their
messaging and communicate their benefits
to customers even though the actual product
offerings are pretty much the same.

Now some of these brand positions have
evolved through the years, so it's important
to update this analysis every year. We will
talk more about this in Chapter Fifteen,
when we discuss the marketing planning

process. It's good to grow as customers grow, so the brand positioning must evolve to stay relevant.

Let's look at one more example to drive the point home (pun intended): cars.

This is a dicey one since there are so many nuances, but it's a good example of how we should try to distill the analysis down to its simplest form to help make a decision. Here it goes:

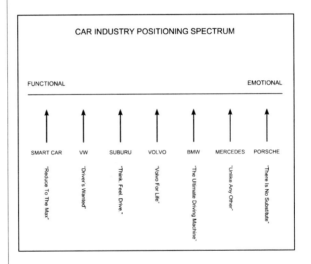

Wow, that was actually hard, but look at the incredible range of car positioning.

Now these are all obviously big blockbuster brands, but there's no reason why we couldn't replicate the process for small businesses. Simply plot the positioning of the competitors onto the positioning spectrum and see where your brand fits.

Great marketers always make sure their brand sits in a unique spot, closer to the emotional end of the spectrum.

If you can't find a place where the brand would fit amidst the competition on the positioning spectrum, then you need to do some homework on how to make the positioning more distinctive and more emotionally connected to the customer.

Now it is time to bring it all home.

9 A Marketing Classic
Pampered and Safe

"If you only do one thing with this book, fill out this format and share it with everyone who works on the business."

Pay close attention here. If there's one thing I want you to do after reading this book, just one thing, it's in this chapter.

We've just been discussing positioning, one of the most elusive of marketing concepts. It trips even the best marketers up. It took me a long time to master it, and I still have to think really hard when I work through it, especially for new brands.

Throughout the book we've been talking about defining the brand, identifying the target market, and outlining the rational and emotional benefits. I hope you've been enjoying it.

Now we are going to tie it all together, and put all of the pieces together so that we can start to craft the Experience Effect for small business.

I'm going to go back probably three decades and use a very classic positioning format. Some people credit a version of it to the classic coffee brand Sanka from the General Foods Company, now owned by Kraft Foods. It's been around that long!

This incredibly simple format takes all the ingredients we've been creating in this book so far, and puts it into context. It's a format that I still use almost every day, because it so clearly distills all of the elements of the brand into one simple flow.

There are many versions of this format, but suffice it to say that all the big brands use one version or another to craft their full positioning statements. By using this one, you will not only be acting like a big brand, you are likely to have much more clarity on the business than ever before, and hopefully more than the competitors.

I call the format "For-Who-Is-That-Because-So-By", sort of like Do-Re-Me in a way.

Here's what it looks like:

FOR:

WHO:

BRAND IS:

THAT:

BECAUSE:

SO:

BEST
EXPRESSED
BY:

The format is like a questionnaire—we just fill in the blanks. It's easy to do because we've been doing the hard work all along.

FOR:	The Target Market (demographically)
WHO:	The Target Market (psychographically)
BRAND IS:	Type of Business
THAT:	Rational Benefit
BECAUSE:	Proof Points (no more than 3)
SO:	Emotional Benefit
BEST EXPRESSED BY:	Tagline

Notice how we have all of these elements all put together already, except for maybe the tagline. Let's pick a brand and try to fill it out.

How about Pampers:

FOR:	new mothers
WHO:	are nervous about caring for their babies
PAMPERS IS:	the ultimate in diaper area protection
THAT:	keeps messy/irritating substances away from baby's skin
BECAUSE:	of a leak-proof barrier that instantly absorbs moisture
SO:	you can spend quality time bonding with your baby
BEST EXPRESSED BY:	Where We Grow Together

Now I have made all of that up (except for the tagline), just for the point of illustration. See how it all comes together within this classic format? Don't you want to write one for your business?

Let's craft one for my favorite dry cleaner that I talked about in Chapter One:

FOR:	our beloved neighbors of Chelsea, New York
WHO:	are the best dressed folks in town
DRY CLEANER IS:	your safe haven for all your dry cleaning needs
THAT:	takes good care of you and your clothes
BECAUSE:	special laundry process and a commitment to care
SO:	you can do the more important things in your life
BEST EXPRESSED BY:	Neighbors Taking Care of Neighbors

I think these are so much fun! Like I said, if you only do one thing with this book, fill out this format and share it with everyone who works on the business.

Do it now, before you even go on to the next chapter. You'll need it.

I just used it today for one of my big clients (a huge blockbuster brand) and also for one of my smaller clients (an entrepreneur). It magically worked for both of them and it will work for you. I know it will. Have at it.

Here's a blank one if you want to try it right now:

FOR:

WHO:

BRAND IS:

THAT:

BECAUSE:

SO:

BEST
EXPRESSED
BY:

I'd like to think that's the best work you've done all day!

10 Reaching Your Customer
Bag It

"Think about a typical day in the life of customers, and consider how and where we can intersect with them during the course of that day."

With our positioning complete, it's time to connect with our customers. You do this every day, I'm sure, but now think about it through the eyes of a marketer. We need to make sure that every interaction with our customers is consistent with the brand positioning we have developed.

We need to make sure that our customers experience our brand purposefully, and we can't do that if we are unable to find them and reach them.

A big time brand manager would start talking about advertising, media planning, production budgets, and airtime. Since we are a small business, we don't have those resources, so we're not going there, but we are going to do some media planning in our own way.

For our purposes, media planning (as in where to place advertising) is really just about getting the brand within arm's reach of the customer—making sure that as our customers go through their day, they see the brand and get a chance to interact with it. The type of interaction doesn't matter at this point it can be an advertisement, packaging, signage, a website, banner ad, tweet, or Facebook post.

Anything that will allow customers to make a connection with the brand.

We basically plan out the media so that we make sure our customers have many opportunities to engage with the brand. The key to a media plan for any size brand is to put the brand in the path of the customer. A media plan consists of all the ways that we can "touch" the customer throughout the day, week, month, or year, whatever the period of time.

I call this a touchpoint—a point at which the brand can touch the customer.

It's a fundamental part of marketing; it's where all the work we've been talking about finally gets to the target market; "show time" shall we say! It's where the marketing execution begins and where the brand experience starts to happen.

A touchpoint can be anything. The big brands use the obvious ones—television advertising, a website, or maybe billboard advertising. Small businesses need to be a bit more clever and creative, since their budgets may not allow for such mass reach.

How do we know when we have a touch-point? Well, if our particular target customer comes in contact with it, then it's a potential touchpoint —at least that's the way that I see it.

Touchpoints come in three basic garden varieties: paid, earned, and owned.

Paid touchpoints are just that: we pay for them. Things like local television advertising, online banner advertising, radio spots, or an outdoor billboard are all examples of paid touchpoints. We pay another company to run our messaging on their vehicle. They own the vehicle, and we pay them to use it.

Earned touchpoints are quite different. We don't pay to get into the medium, so we have to earn our way in with interesting content and engagement. There may still be some cost associated with these, but it's generally just development cost, not the cost to a third party to manage and run it.

Public relations is a common example of an earned touchpoint—we convince an editor to run a story about our brand. Our efforts have earned their attention and they write a story about our brand in a unique and compelling way.

The world of earned touchpoints has exploded. Social media, for the most part, is earned. We can build a Facebook page and update it regularly—if it's compelling then people come to it. We've earned their interest. The same can be said for Twitter. If a local business gets a local radio DJ to talk about the brand, then that could be considered an earned touchpoint as well, if in fact it's compelling enough to get listeners.

Of course some touchpoints can be paid and earned. Facebook, for example is largely earned, but we can also buy Facebook ads that are paid.

I hope I'm not confusing the point! Earned touchpoints are much more cost effective, and I would generally say that they are a better resource for small business, just on budget alone. Earned touchpoints can also be more meaningful in many cases as well, because they feel more real and sincere. They come with an endorsement, in a way.

We also have all the touchpoints within our business itself. All the materials we generate, the office or retail space, the website, and all of the employee interactions with customers, these are touchpoints as well. The difference is that we "own" these outright, no third party involvement. They are what I call owned touchpoints.

Owned touchpoints are all within our control, so we should always maximize our use of them. Customer service touchpoints; whether on the phone, in person, on the website, or in social media are all owned touchpoints, and very important owned touchpoints I might add.

I always recommend a mix of the three kinds of touchpoints (paid, earned, owned) to maximize the reach to customers and to be efficient with the budget.

When thinking through potential touchpoints, remember that sometimes the medium alone can also give the brand credibility. Running a television ad certainly makes a brand feel more important however; it doesn't mean it will produce results so choose wisely.

As we start the process of building the brand experience, let's start to brainstorm all of the possible ways we can intersect with our customers in their lives. Let's list out all the potential touchpoints whether they are paid, earned, or owned.

At this point in time, don't worry if they are the best choices, just list out all of the possibilities.

Think about a typical day in the life of customers, and think about how and where we can intersect with them during the course of that day. Then we'll expand to a week, a month, or even a year—to make sure that we've captured all the possibilities.

Concentrate on the ones that are the most actionable—don't bother listing broadcast advertising if it's not even a possibility for the business.

Are there certain times of the day, or the month, or even the year when customers can more easily come in contact with a brand message? Don't evaluate the ideas yet, just brainstorm them and list them out. Think through seasonality as well, since certain times of the year offer more options.

Don't even think about whether they are paid, earned, or owned yet, just list them out.

Let's say we run a small dress shop, catering to the more formal clothing needs of women. Our customers range in age from 16 to 55, but have one common goal—they are all going to a formal party—so we have a range of dresses that fit age and occasion needs.

Let's pick two of our core customers whom we would have created a customer collage for in Chapter Seven: an 18 year-old-girl going to her high school Senior Prom and a 38-year-old going to a charity event.

Let's list out the touchpoints for each of them.

For the 18-year-old high school girl:

- Facebook, Foursquare

- Mobile texting

- School bus (yes, some places are allowing advertising on the side of school buses)

- Radio (certain times of the day)

- Outdoor billboards (after all, she is likely to be driving now)

- Transit advertising

- Online banner ads on certain websites

- Online gaming

- Xbox, Nintendo, etc (women are big gamers, believe it or not, even teenage girls—so it is not just for the boys)

This is a good example of where seasonality plays a very big role in listing out touchpoints for certain businesses. Teenagers are generally only interested in formal attire during prom season so think through the touchpoints that are in play during that time of the year. Don't waste your time at other periods—the target customer is not in the right mindset to make it efficient for the budget.

The striking fact here, even as I write the list out myself, is that there are not so many! 18-year-old girls are hard to reach, at least for small business. It's not like we are going to advertise on the CW television network to reach them. We need to be smarter and more creative, more local, more specific. I would say that most of the touchpoints are online or on a mobile phone. We could also think through where teenage girls hang out in the local area and list those as possible touchpoints as well.

Let's try a few more:

- Local coffee shops and restaurants (small businesses helping each other reach the same customer)

- Bloggers (especially fashion bloggers who write about prom season, particularly if they live in the area)

- Word of mouth recommendations (perhaps generated through local media via public relations outreach)

- Refer a friend coupons

This is hard! Let's get even more clever:

- Shopping bags (yes, even the store's shopping bag is an owned touchpoint because it gets carried around town like a billboard advertisement after a purchase)

- Clothing tags (nice reinforcement at the point of purchase)

- Sidewalks and parking lots, particularly close to the store

- Schools (maybe the administrators will allow a fashion show for prom)

- Shoe stores (perhaps negotiate some joint marketing programs where again small businesses can help each other reach the same customer)

I'd like to make a comment about shopping bags—it's one of my favorite things in marketing life. I am all about the bag. If you have any kind of a retail business, then think hard about the shopping bag. It's your brand!

For retail outlets, shopping bags are a powerful owned touchpoint and a major part of the brand experience. Think about it, it's a billboard that gets carried around from the time the customer walks out the door, to the time she steps inside her home. And even once home, it's the "packaging" that reinforces a good purchase decision. I am always so impressed by businesses that put a lot of thought into their shopping bags.

It's a sign to me that they "get it".

Now if the brand is "green" and shopping bags don't make sense, then that's part of the brand as well. That's great because it's better to be consistent, but I would still recommend thinking through alternate packaging options to the shopping bag, like perhaps a reusable version.

Living in New York City, I see the importance of shopping bags every day. The bags truly become walking billboards and serve as reminders to others walking down the street of the popularity of the brand. They announce sales, they remind us to run errands, and they inspire us to go pick up something cool for a night out.

Paul Smith, Barney's, and Banana Republic do a great job of using shopping bags as touchpoints. When there's a sale going on at any of these stores, we all know about it for blocks and blocks. The streets are blanketed with shoppers walking around with their sale merchandise, and it totally gets the rest of us motivated to go check out the bargains.

It's a valuable lesson that should be learned by small businesses—use a great shopping bag if it's relevant to the customer.

Packaging in any form is an important "owned" touchpoint and a key ingredient in the brand experience.

One of my favorite examples of a more creative touchpoint is something that I've noticed from Zappos, the online retailer known best for shoes. When we go through security at the airport, we obviously now have to take off our shoes. Well Zappos put inserts into each of the trays where we put our shoes as a not-so-subtle reminder that maybe it's time to get some new shoes. It is unexpected, yet so relevant, and totally in keeping with the brand.

I'm also betting that air travelers are also more savvy online, which makes sense for the brand to use this paid touchpoint. Zappos decided to hit customers at a time when they were taking off their shoes, and perhaps self-conscious about it, with a message to replace those shoes with something new. This touchpoint is nothing short of brilliant.

Now let's go back to the dress shop we've been discussing, and continue our touchpoint brainstorm with the other target customer, the adult woman going to a special event:

- Local television news

- Email

- Drive time radio

- Local newspaper

- Facebook, Twitter, Foursquare

- Outdoor billboards

- Transit advertising

- Mobile texting

Notice that some of these touchpoints are the same across both target markets, and some are different. That's ok, there should be some cross over because that will make our marketing more efficient. In terms of prioritizing, we may actually use that as criteria: only choose touchpoints that hit all target markets.

But for now, we are just brainstorming so we are not crossing anything off the list quite yet.

There are many touchpoints that may not seem to be touchpoints that we should also consider. Some only hit current customers, but that's ok. We are developing a brand experience for them too, so we should include all brand touchpoints, even the ones that just reach our current customers.

Everything about the brand is a touchpoint. I mentioned shopping bags, but you should also consider these owned touchpoints as well:

- Company receptionist

- Signage

- Tablecloths and menus (if you are a restaurant)

- Brochures

- Business cards

- Mobile phone covers

- Email signatures

- Voicemail messages

Anything that a customer can see as part of the brand is a touchpoint and needs to be considered. Even the pens used in meetings are a touchpoint, and don't forget the pads of paper. Some even say that the type of laptop you use is a touchpoint to some degree. Are you a MAC user or a PC user, and what does that say about your brand?

I can tell you that I made a very conscious decision about it.

The brainstorm list of touchpoints should include anything and everything that comes in contact with your customer—paid, earned, or owned—just list them all out.

With a long brainstorm list in hand, it's time to start making some decisions.

Chapter 10: Reaching Your Customer

11 Mapping Touchpoints
Proud as a Peacock

"Don't choose a touchpoint that is inconsistent with the brand essence."

We've listed out all of the potential ways to reach our target customer, so now it's time to start making some decisions.

I always say that good marketers are good decision makers, and here's another area that counts. While most of those touchpoints we listed in the last chapter could be viable, there's no way that we could execute all of them. There's simply not enough time and resources. That's true of the big brands, and it's certainly true for small businesses too.

So what does a big brand do at this stage in developing a marketing plan?

Big brands make decisions, they prioritize, and they cut the list down to identify only the most effective touchpoints. The Chief Marketing Officer (CMO) of a big brand will take a look at that list that we generated, and will pick the touchpoints that are the most impactful at reaching and engaging the brand's specific customers.

This is easy to say, but not so easy to do.

Don't worry—we've been doing our homework and following a simple process of creating a compelling brand experience. We know who we are as a business, as a real brand. We understand who are customers are and how they live their lives.

We've even been tracking the competition so we understand everything that other businesses are doing to talk to the same customers that we are trying to attract.

All of this information (the brand, the customer, and the competition) merges to form the brand's positioning as we discussed in Chapters Eight and Nine, and it is the positioning that will help us pick the right touchpoints.

With positioning in hand, simply go back through the brainstorm list and choose the touchpoints that make the most sense. It'll be quite easier than you might think.

As we've already mentioned, we can cut the list simply by eliminating the touchpoints that don't reach all of our target markets. If in fact we have more than one set of customers, as in the dress shop scenario where we talked about using touchpoints that targeted both teenagers for prom season as well as adult women for special events.

We can also prioritize on other dimensions as well like affordability, ease of execution, and size of the audience that will be reached there. We should also choose touchpoints that have the closest proximity to our brand essence. In other words, those that are most "like" our brand.

This is perhaps the most important criterion: don't choose a touchpoint that is inconsistent with the brand essence. It will end up confusing customers.

For example, we wouldn't want to advertise feminine hygiene products in the men's locker room at gyms around the country or a wholesome line of snacks on a billboard on the Vegas strip. We also would never use a lot of digital touchpoints if digital doesn't make sense for the brand (I can't honestly imagine that, but hopefully you get the point).

Go back to the touchpoints and just rank them in priority order of most important, most easily executed, and fastest to get to market. Put them on one document to see how it all flows.

As we mentioned in the last chapter, the big brands call this a media plan or a channel plan, meaning a list of all the ways that the brand will reach customers through various media outlets or channels.

Create a flowchart to see how all the touchpoints come together—or what I call a touchpoint tree. This touchpoint tree makes everything so much more visual. In fact, let's do just that—visualize it. Let's draw a touchpoint tree as a reminder of the decisions we've made to reach our customers and connect with them.

A touchpoint tree could look like this:

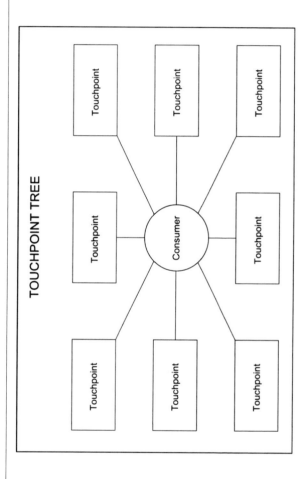

Some of the touchpoints we could add could be:

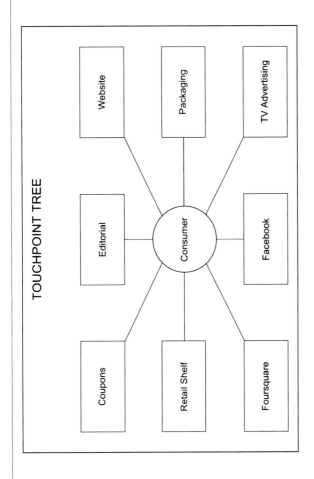

TOUCHPOINT TREE

Website

Packaging

TV Advertising

Editorial

Consumer

Facebook

Coupons

Retail Shelf

Foursquare

And for our dress shop, it could look like this:

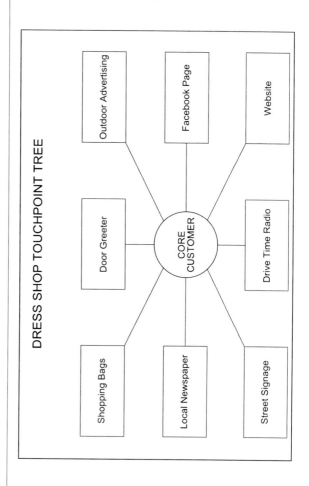

DRESS SHOP TOUCHPOINT TREE

Outdoor Advertising

Facebook Page

Website

Door Greeter

CORE CUSTOMER

Drive Time Radio

Shopping Bags

Local Newspaper

Street Signage

I believe this will help sort all the touchpoints out and keep them consistent with the brand. Let's take a look at a great brand as inspiration for when we prioritize our list.

NBC is a major television network and it does an amazing job of "being there" every time I turn around. You may not have thought about NBC as a brand, but trust me, it is. NBC markets the network and the shows and the news formats like nobody's business.

If I consciously stop and think about it, NBC touches me all day long with brand messaging that clearly gets in my face. I watch *The Today Show* in the morning, and I am on NBC properties online all day long, including msnbc.com. When I hop in a taxi, there's taxi TV that is all NBC programming.

Get on board a plane, and it's NBC in-flight. Outdoor billboard ads promote their shows, especially *The Today Show*. Trailers run all day long on the network promoting the upcoming shows for the week. I follow the network on Twitter to get little news clips all day long, thereby keeping me in the loop of what's happening in the world. The NBC brand provides celebrity news, real news, financial updates, and entertainment all day long, every single day.

NBC clearly has a media plan, or a touch-point tree, to reach their customers/viewers like me. The brand reaches me all day long in a relevant way; therefore I remain a loyal consumer of its programming. Let's face it; we can switch channels and Twitter feeds at a moment's notice, so it's even more important for the NBC brand to stay relevant in a consumer's mind.

The NBC touchpoint tree might look something like this:

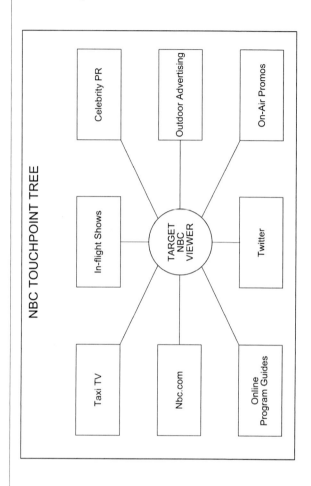

The NBC touchpoint tree is consistent at each turn, yet tailored to be appropriate to the relevant medium, regardless of whether it is broadcast television, outdoor advertising, website, or social media. The brand's touchpoint tree is beautifully executed.

You too can do the same on a local level with your small business. You just need a good touchpoint tree. Start by making some decisions about the touchpoints identified and choose the ones that make sense. Then we'll need to activate them!

12 Activating Touchpoints
Let the Force Be with You

"The magic comes from finding the right balance."

Now that we have mapped out our touchpoints, it's time to activate them. It is time to bring them to life, and to craft our messaging at each and every one of them, one at a time.

The big brands have agencies that do this for them, often multiple agencies that each specifically work on their own touchpoints. Advertising agencies do the television and print advertising, digital agencies do the websites, public relations agencies get key placements, and so on. Even special promotion agencies do couponing and retail displays.

The teams for each of these agencies are huge.

We don't have those resources, but we can still do just as good a job, because we have many of the same tools.

The key is to take each touchpoint, one by one, and decide what we want the brand message to be at that moment. We have to decide what we want to say to our customers at each interaction. It should be the same, but tailored to each touchpoint, and always consistent with the brand.

The big advertising agencies write a "creative brief" for their clients to help guide the process. We don't need to do that necessarily, but we should answer a few fundamental questions when creating messaging at each touchpoint:

- Why is the customer at that touchpoint?

- How can the brand add value to customers at that touchpoint?

- What's the role of that touchpoint compared to other touchpoints that are mapped out?

- What can the brand do and say within that touchpoint?

In other words, if we had chosen Facebook ads in our touchpoint tree, then we would have to answer those questions to decide how our brand wants to use Facebook to engage with our customers. So we would have to answer:

- Why are our customers on Facebook? It's probably to connect with family and friends from throughout the years.

Chapter 12: Activating Touchpoints

- How can the brand add value to customers by using Facebook ads? Maybe give a money saving coupon as an incentive to "like" the brand.

- What's the role of Facebook ads as part of the touchpoint tree? Perhaps to find friends of friends who have similar profiles that might be interested in the brand?

- What can the brand do and say on Facebook ads? There are very specific requirements about visuals and word count for Facebook ads that we have to follow.

Knowing all of this, we can now craft our messaging and our visual imagery for Facebook ads, as an example. Then we can continue down the line of our touchpoint tree, executing each touchpoint, one by one.

We want to make sure that at each interaction we are answering those questions or whatever else is relevant. These questions are a simplified version of what the big agencies use in their creative briefs, but they will get us a long way toward creating a great experience at each touchpoint.

One of the fundamentals of an amazing brand experience is to keep the messaging consistent at each touchpoint. We want to say the same kinds of things in the same kind of manner at each touchpoint, so that customers' perceptions of the brand are consistent along the way.

Consistency is a key tenant of achieving the Experience Effect, particularly for a small business whose resources are limited.

An equally important fundamental for creating a remarkable brand experience is making sure that the brand messaging and brand experience is tailored to the touchpoint. The brand messaging and brand experience should be tailored to why the customer is at that touchpoint.

Therefore, if we are building a website, then we need to make sure that we tailor the brand message to what customers are looking for from a website. That may be very different than the messaging that's appropriate for a print ad, or a text message.

The big brands have large teams dedicated to producing the marketing at each touchpoint, but small businesses don't, and that's a disadvantage. But that's where we also have a big advantage because it will be a lot easier to keep consistency throughout the touchpoints we choose to market. There are not as many people, opinions, and interpretations to manage, and we can just focus on making sure that the messaging is clear and consistent. A smaller team though, means limited resources, so we have to focus.

Pick the most important touchpoints and pour the resources into those. If a website is vital to the business, then make the best website that money can buy for the customer. Give customers exactly what they need at that touchpoint, and exactly what they are looking for. Be sure to build the best website possible before moving onto the next touchpoint.

Creating an optimal brand experience requires a lot of work. It's a complicated balance of being armed with the right information, and crafting the right brand message, along with the right mix of being consistent yet tailored at each touchpoint.

It's the consistency part that often troubles people. Many think that consistency means being exactly the same, to the letter of the law, at every touchpoint, but that really wouldn't work either because then we're not maximizing the effectiveness of the touchpoint.

We wouldn't put the same message in a tweet as we would in an email campaign, right?

At the other extreme, tailoring each touchpoint can cause a lot of inconsistency. If we tailor too much, then the brand can get lost or look different at each interaction.

The magic comes from finding the right balance. This is what separates the great marketers from the less successful ones. This is what separates great brands from little known products.

One great example of a tailored touchpoint is Best Buy's Twelpforce initiative, which used Twitter as a convenient, on-trend customer service tool. Sure Best Buy is a huge brand, but we can easily replicate what the brand did with Twitter for small business. It didn't cost much money at all, but Best Buy maximized the touchpoint, using it differently than all the other touchpoints, to get success. Let me give you a little background.

Best Buy was having a business problem, trying to compete with other electronics retailers on price, selection, and service. It did not appear to be winning. It got into the game of focusing on price, since that's where shoppers focus, which is a tricky game to play because it affects profit margin and really does nothing to improve brand loyalty. It's very difficult to market around price because it doesn't differentiate and it's so easily copied—even Walmart has had its struggles.

Best Buy determined that maybe it could get out of the pricing war by improving service. Selection wasn't going to be a way to win either, since virtually every retailer has nearly the same selection, so the Best Buy brand decided to up the ante in service.

Now the company had already acquired Geek Squad, an at-home service for installing and repairing electronics. Geek Squad had become a bit of a phenomenon since it was one of the first in the market. I even used the service a few times and it was quite good, but expensive, and not everyone would want to use the service, especially for little requests. The brand could certainly do more, and needed to do more to win in the electronics retailing business.

The company decided to try something else to give a greater number of their customers more access to good service. It created Twelpforce—a new way of providing quick and efficient service to customers on Twitter, before and after their purchases.

The company solicited an entire group of employees who were already using Twitter to basically start tweeting for the brand to help customers with service issues. When customers bought a new item, they were told that they could tweet any questions or problems they were having and someone from Twelpforce would help them, almost instantly. The team did an amazing job, almost instantly.

The concept was brilliant—rather than Twitter becoming just another advertising venue for the brand, pumping out the exact same messages as with television or print, it became a customer service touchpoint.

The brand's reputation soared as customers started to talk about how great the service was at Best Buy. That's what's so great about social media, people talk and share!

The employees loved it too, because many of them enjoyed being on Twitter so this gave them a voice there. Many of the post-purchase blues that come from making a big purchase (buyer's regret) could now be eliminated with great service through social media.

Don't know where the blue cord plugs in? Just send a tweet to Twelpforce. Missing the instructions manual? Just send a tweet to Twelpforce.

So what did the brand do next? It started to advertise Twelpforce and began to use it as a way to differentiate the brand from its competitors. The brand started pulling in other touchpoints to support it.

Twelpforce is a perfect example of a touchpoint, and its use is very different than other touchpoints in the marketing plan. It has been so effective that it improved the business. Isn't that why we do marketing?

There is no reason why we can't do the same in small business. No reason at all. It doesn't cost a dime to use Twitter, and there's no technology curve. If you don't know how to use it, ask a friend how and in a matter of two hours you'll be proficient enough to start taking action.

There are even some short books on the subject of maximizing Twitter for businesses and brands.

Once you have figured out how to use Twitter, tell customers about it. Use it as a way to start an ongoing dialogue with them. Send them updates and offers, and give them news of what's going on in the industry. Keep them connected by giving them information that they can't easily get from other places. Add value to their lives.

You'll have much more loyal customers as a result, and they will integrate the brand into their day. You will be filling their needs and their wants.

I know I do it. I have many customers, suppliers, employees, and colleagues that I communicate with on Twitter and Facebook. It's an effective tool to stay connected and to solve problems.

Remember that little dress shop example from the last few chapters? I had an interesting experience during my daughter's prom season this year at a local dress shop in my small town in Pennsylvania. As we were selecting dresses to try on, the shop owner was checking her Facebook page to see if anyone else from the same high school had already bought any of the dresses. She was helping to make sure my daughter would be the only one in her favorite dress at the prom.

Now that's using social media to add value to the customer and to maximize the shopping experience.

Use Best Buy (a huge brand) and my little dress shop example (a small business) as inspiration for how you can improve your small business marketing.

See you online!

13 Navigating the Digital World
Talent Online

"We are only there because they've invited us in, so don't abuse the privilege."

If the example of Best Buy and Twelpforce from the last chapter didn't convince you, then I am going to keep trying here. The digital space should be your greatest asset when marketing your small business.

Anyone in marketing will tell you that the digital revolution (yes, it is a revolution) has completely changed how brands communicate to customers. Scratch that, "with" customers. We now talk "with" our customers via social media, not just "at" them via advertising.

I have been around long enough to see the entire digital evolution, from the first time we used email, to initial websites, to email campaigns, to microsites, to banner advertising, to social media, and a little thing called Facebook.

It's a revolution that has not stopped.

To try to keep up with the technology is a full time job in and of itself. So don't try—just focus on the marketing part.

It's important to recognize that digital marketing truly is a small business owner's best friend. Truly. So while it may be hard to stay on top of the technology curve, you can and should stay abreast of how to use digital vehicles to market your brand.

Much of the digital space is very cost efficient and timely, and that's the best part. Even the big brands recognize the inconvenience of planning months ahead of time to create a very expensive television commercial that is then virtually impossible to change if you decide that something isn't working perfectly. They have the budgets for it, but I think they are losing the patience.

This is not true in the digital space.

Development costs are a fraction of traditional budgets and although there may be a build time involved, the ability to change on the fly makes it a marketer's dream. Digital marketing comes with not only the ability to evolve and to continually improve, but also the ability to customize for specific customers. Personalization and customization is a huge benefit of digital marketing.

We can now engage with our customers like never before from a personal perspective.

It's incredible, actually. We've never been this fortunate as marketers. It's an exciting time and I embrace it. I love the change that technology brings and I love trying new things. You should too—your customers will appreciate it.

That doesn't mean that the digital world is easy.

The big brands have the resources and the desire to analyze every waking digital moment of their customer segments and they have vast IT departments that can tweak each piece of marketing communication. You don't have these same luxuries, so it's important to make really smart decisions about how to use digital marketing to connect with customers and create a brand experience.

We are going to start, once again, with the customer.

Advancements in technology and digital assets have completely changed how we all live our lives. Particularly how we research information and communicate with each other. It seems like I rarely talk to anyone anymore—at least live anyway! But I feel connected to my friends from every aspect of my life like never before.

You can do the same with your customers.

Technology has changed how we drive, how we buy, how we learn, how we discover, and how we make decisions. Take a look at the doctor's office. We sometimes know more about what we are experiencing than our doctors because we are more in tune with our bodies now that we have knowledge. This knowledge may be information we pulled from the internet to try to find out what's going on. We also might use this knowledge to fill in the gaps of information that the doctor leaves out.

From our perspective here, though, the internet and digital technology has also changed how we interact with brands—for the big brands and certainly for small businesses. Back in the day, we would find out about a brand from a television commercial. Then as retailers got more powerful, sometimes we would find out about a brand from seeing it in a store. Now, often our first interaction with a brand is online, and usually we first hear about a brand online from someone else who has experienced it before us.

It's true of the big brands, and I believe that it is also true of many small businesses. Unless you are a local business that people literally walk by every day, most likely many of your interactions with customers are somehow online, or certainly could be—and it's the online experience that potentially keeps the relationship with customers going.

When I was trying to find a designer to help us plan our new space at the agency, I went online. Well first I asked around for some recommendations, but then I immediately went online. I examined all of the online portfolios and checked references. I made my decision before ever meeting anyone. The physical meeting just reinforced the decision that I had already made online.

The same is true for hiring talent at the agency. When recruiting for art directors or copywriters, I go online. I look at portfolios and read examples of their work. I choose new talent based on what I see in the digital world.

I also see how active they are on Facebook and Twitter, because if they are going to work at the agency then they better know social media. I also like to see how they behave! You can do the same for hiring talent and also for scouting out potential customers, depending on the business.

I have a theory that social media, for many brands, has become THE brand experience. If you think about it, for the big brands in many ways it's only through Facebook or Twitter that we really hear from the brand. It is where we really talk with the brand. Granted, it's through a community manager who has been hired to talk to us, but we are still communicating directly with the brand, thereby making the brand more human.

I wrote a blog post about a major home goods brand and within hours I had a tweet from "Ryan" from the brand thanking me for the comments. The brand has a voice, the voice of Ryan who was quite charming and consistent with the brand I must say. I felt quite satisfied.

So how do small businesses take advantage of all of this?

Don't try to do it all at once. Start with the big social media outlets, and work your way through the digital and social media sites that you think will be the most beneficial to your small business.

Start with Facebook. This is a place for friends, family members, and your biggest "fans" to come and listen to what you have to say about your business. For regular Facebook pages, there is a cap to the number of people who can friend you, so you may want to consider creating a "public figure" page, which allows a virtual unlimited number of people to "like" you.

You should think of your Facebook page as a place where your closest "friends" will come, because they want to hear about you. You can post pictures, give updates on the business, and even offer promotional incentives for your best customers.

Facebook is all about loyalty.

LinkedIn, on the other hand, is all about professional networking. You will want to create a professional profile on this site to connect with all the people you have come in contact with professionally throughout the year. This is a place for colleagues and for finding business contacts through the colleagues that you know.

Twitter is all about thought leadership, so you'll want to have a Twitter presence so that you can talk about the industry. Twitter allows you to follow people that you may not know, but that you admire. Give your opinions on what's going on in your world, and others will follow you too. Twitter is about having a voice in what you do. It's also a great place for news, where you can catch up in an instant on what's going on. We all know that news is breaking on Twitter far faster than on other forms of media.

For me, YouTube is about pop culture.

This is the place you can go to catch up on what's going on in entertainment. I don't have a lot of time for television and music anymore, so YouTube is how I stay connected. If I hear about a new video or tv show, I can get a segment of it on YouTube and keep in touch with what's going on.

Foursquare is location-based, allowing customers to "check in" when they arrive places to share their whereabouts or to collect special offers from those locales. If you rely on local traffic, then you may want to investigate Foursquare.

Coupon sites like Groupon and LivingSocial are certainly hitting stride, adding real marketing value for local businesses. If you think the brand is at all promotionally sensitive and you rely on the local market, then definitely check out these social couponing sites.

Just be careful not to use them too much, you don't want couponing to be overly associated with your brand.

Of course there is also Google+, which took off like no one could have ever expected. I personally use Google+ to have a place for a smaller and more personal network of my friends, but that's just me. It's another social media outlet that actually has a lot of functionality. Check it out as well.

This is a sampling of the big social media outlets, and there are certainly others. I recommend that you start with these, and then move from here to expand your online presence. Again, the key is how you use these outlets. Don't try to do everything all the time. Keep it simple or you will never get fully engaged.

Remember that any of them can be a great vehicle for learning about your target customer and your competition.

YouTube is easy, just start out by watching and monitoring. You don't even have to "register." There is no need quite yet to do a lot more. When you get in the game deeper, you can eventually build your own YouTube channel with personalized video content—although unless you are into consulting and public speaking it may not be necessary.

LinkedIn is just a matter of making a profile and then connecting with other people—not too complicated. Creating a profile is like writing your resume again. Simply follow the steps as the site literally walks you through the inputs.

Facebook and Twitter are the two sites where you will be the most active. Facebook and Twitter are where you want to create a brand experience. A constant stream of communication on these two huge social media sites will engage your customers and help to build your business. Concentrate marketing efforts into making the brand's presence exceptionally powerful here.

Once you are on these sites, it's time to create a content calendar.

This is something we do for our clients all the time. We literally write out the content and the messaging that we want to distribute to our "likes" and "followers" each day. Day-by-day, month-by-month, perhaps even for the entire year. We plan out what we are going to post so that we know it's going to be interesting, engaging, and consistent over time. We also decide in advance how often we are going to post and how we are going to mix the messaging between interesting content, facts about the brand, and promotional offers.

We try to mix it up so that it stays interesting. There's nothing worse than a person who only talks about himself—same is true of a brand that only talks about itself. I would recommend alternating between promotional offers, brand messages, and industry content. Keep it continually rotated and fresh so that customers stay engaged.

If it's only about coupons, then customers will print and leave.

Of course, all of this content needs to be written in a way that's consistent with the brand. We don't want to suddenly have a different voice in social media, because it will confuse customers.

If you are doing the actual content management and posting, it'll be easy to stay in the brand "voice." But if you are having someone else do it (like "Ryan") then it's important that they know all about the brand, the positioning, and the customer. Make sure they are educated on what we've been talking about in this entire book, and ensure that their posts are appropriately aligned with the brand and with the customer.

With this as a base, we can start to use social media as a way to network. Sure, we want to keep current customers engaged, but we also want to attract new ones. Start networking online to find new contacts and new resources. Use sites like LinkedIn to find people who have similar interests and backgrounds, or to reconnect with old colleagues.

How you will use social media to network will depend largely on your business, but in many cases LinkedIn can be a big help—especially for lead generation and recruiting. It's digital magic of the networking kind. I can find people I know who know people I want to know. You know?

The digital world is also good for customer outreach. We can interact with customers individually if we need to. We can capture their information and then truly establish a one-on-one relationship with them. I connect continually with many of my clients on Twitter, Facebook, and LinkedIn (all three actually).

It takes our relationship to a new level.

We also talked about how we can use digital resources to learn about our competitors and our customers. This kind of research is very effective and basically free. Simply look at the social media presence and the websites of your competitors and observe how they talk to their customers. Discover who among your competitors is engaging successfully in a dialogue with customers and what you can do to mimic the same results.

It's enlightening.

Because our customers are already there in social media, we can meet them live and in person, every single day if it's appropriate. The ultimate power of social media is the ability to establish and maintain a relationship with customers on a continual basis.

We've never been able to do that before as marketers.

Be careful not to bombard or stalk them. Remember that social media is "their" space. We are only there because they've invited us in, so don't abuse the privilege. Our customers can easily opt right out. In fact the biggest reason why customers "break up" with a brand on Facebook or Twitter is because they get bombarded with messages that they don't want or need—so they check out.

Remember that we are there to establish a relationship with our customers and to find new ones. Respect them and engage them and they will become loyal.

Hopefully this has given you the motivation you need to get started in the digital world, or to ramp up your activity. The best way to engage is to dive head first into the endless pool of social media. None of us knew how to use these sites until we started using them, so I encourage you to do the same.

Don't let the technology intimidate you, because it's not about the technology it's about how you engage with people on these sites. If you need help getting started, I'd recommend asking a young adult or a teenager to give you some help. They are not afraid of technology and they can get you up to speed quickly.

If you still need more help, there are a number of books that will give you very prac- tical, in-depth, step-by-step advice. There are also a number of consultants who have set up shop to help small businesses navigate social media. Just do a Google search and you'll find them. They are also easily found on Twitter. There they can give you lots of advice, 140 characters at a time.

Sounds funny, but it can be very helpful.

Once again, my best advice is to just jump in. Create your social media profiles and start sending out messages. You'll figure out what to do. It's a lot of fun.

14 Benchmark Brands
Put It On Ice

"Being a benchmark brand comes from excellence in brand positioning."

I introduced this concept in a blog post that ended up soaring in readership, and I've been talking about it to clients, at conferences, and in the NYU classroom, ever since.

Benchmark brands and default brands.

I just love the notion of being a benchmark brand instead of a default brand. A default brand is a brand that is in your life, almost, well, by default. It's there every day, but you don't really remember how or know why.

While this could be considered the ultimate in brand loyalty, it really isn't. It's passive and a bit lazy.

Using a brand by default is not a conscious decision every day; it's just easier. No thought has to go into a constant choice. Now, there are aspects of being a default brand that from a marketing perspective are amazing, because being in customers' lives is the ultimate goal, right?

Isn't it a sign of loyalty?

Sure, but the problem is that default brands are prone to becoming extinct. All it will take is for another brand to come along and open up a dialogue. The only thing a competitor has to do is to suddenly make it a much more conscious, better choice and suddenly the new brand becomes more relevant than the default brand. This new brand is offering something better than the default brand—establishing a richer relationship with the customer and potentially a much stronger bond.

As a marketer, I don't want to be a default brand, I want more. I want to build an Experience Effect that makes me a benchmark brand.

I want to be engaged with my customers. I want to know them and for them to know me. I want them to make a conscious choice every single day to keep me in their life. I want an active, dynamic relationship with my customers. I want to mean something. I want my positioning to be firmly implanted in their heads, and a conscious part of their lives.

I want to be a benchmark brand. Being a benchmark brand is where it's at—the holy grail of a great brand experience. Being a benchmark brand means being the one that sets the standard for the category, instantly communicating that it's the best of the best. It is essentially the gold standard.

Here's an example. When I walk into a party and I see ice buckets filled with Veuve Cliquot champagne, I instantly know that the host has gone all out and that it's going to be a fun night. In this case, at least for me, Veuve Cliquot is a benchmark brand at that point. The host took the time to pick an amazing brand and put it on ice for me. I appreciate the effort and look forward to returning the favor. Veuve Cliquot is a benchmark brand in this case. For other people, it might be Absolut vodka in this case, or a specific brand of beer.

The ultimate benchmark brand for me? It's a size 30 pair of Diesel jeans—my skinny jeans as they say. Fitting into those jeans symbolizes fit and trim and stylish and young (even though I'm not really any of those things anymore!). Diesel for me is a benchmark brand.

Not all benchmark brands are about fashion and style, though, and they are not all about high prices either.

Tide might be a benchmark brand for you—the brand you choose every time you wash clothes because you firmly believe there is none better. Your mom taught you how to do the laundry and you know what works from your experiences with her. You associate Tide with clean clothes and taking care of your family and the values that your mom taught you. Tide is your benchmark brand in laundry, and you choose it every day.

If you notice, benchmark brands are filled with emotion.

Benchmark brands are those brands that have established such stature in their customers' minds that emotionally, they could never be replaced. They are important beyond reason and beyond functionality. They are brands that have reached the pinnacle with an emotional positioning.

Just because a brand becomes a benchmark brand doesn't mean it keeps that title for life. Benchmark status can get lost a lot quicker than it gets earned.

Look for example at the oil giant BP which was once considered the future of energy—beyond petroleum. The brand sourced from friendly countries and invested a lot of money into new energy research. It was a benchmark in the oil business. A disaster in the Gulf of Mexico and a perceived inadequate response changed the game and their stature over night.

One man's benchmark brand isn't necessarily another man's.

Being a benchmark brand to someone also means the brand has done very careful targeting. Diesel is a benchmark brand for me but I know many men my age that could care less about Diesel. The brand is not even on their radar. For other men, the benchmark brand in clothing might be Lacoste.

For me, though, Lacoste is a default brand—I throw it on when I don't want to really think very hard about what I'm wearing and it could be any brand of "polo" shirt as far as I am concerned. It was probably a gift from someone along the way and I have no problem wearing it. Do I consciously choose it as my look? No, I wear the brand by default on days I just need to throw something on. I've got plenty of them in my closet.

Depending on the customer, a brand might be a benchmark brand, a default brand, something in between, or no perceived brand at all. It varies by the user and their experiences, expectations, and mindset.

Tide is only a benchmark brand to those who are emotionally connected to it. Truly defining and understanding the customer is part of the process of becoming a benchmark brand, and building an ongoing, consistent Experience Effect is how a brand keeps that status over time.

So what can be learned from these big, illustrious benchmark brands?

Excellence. Being a benchmark brand comes from excellence in brand positioning, customer understanding, and choosing and executing touchpoints—excellence in all forms of marketing. A benchmark brand delivers excellence every step of the way, consistently over time.

You too can become a benchmark brand for your customers, and in fact that should be the ultimate goal.

If you are in real estate, then you can become the benchmark realtor in your area. You can become the one agent whose real estate specialization excels beyond comparison to others in the market. You can be the benchmark realtor that keeps customers coming over and over again for buying and selling their homes—for consultation in all matters in real estate.

I have a benchmark hair salon in New York. I wouldn't go anywhere else because they know me and my hair (and if you know me, you know my hair is muy importante to me). They actively engage with me every single time I go in. They discuss my hair, talk about my options. The gentleman who styles (notice I said "styles") my hair literally pulls each curl out one at a time and individually cuts it. He knows how tricky my hair is, or at least that's how he makes me feel. It's not the same old, same old every time, everyone there actively engages with me during every visit. This hair salon is my benchmark brand.

I think in some ways it's easier for small businesses to establish a benchmark. You can get closer to your customers than most of the big brands. You have the ability to really get to know your customers, and to service them beyond compare. You can tailor your messaging to them, and in some cases your offerings. You can live their lives right along with them, as a part of their community, figuratively (or should I say "digitally") speaking.

Being a benchmark brand also means utilizing touchpoints to their maximum potential. If you want to be a benchmark brand and you need to be on Twitter, then you need to send out the best tweets possible.

It's very rewarding to be the benchmark brand, kind of like The Academy Awards of marketing. Be the benchmark in your business, for your customers. It'll keep you invested in the business and will keep the customers coming back for more.

15 The Three-Year Plan
Lessons, Learned

So I ask you, "What did you learn this year?"

Becoming a benchmark brand takes a lot of work. It is part inspiration, and part perspiration, as we talked about earlier. It takes a lot of vision and planning—and a true commitment to executing continued excellence.

If you are a small business owner, chances are you are also an entrepreneur. You've done what you need to, when you need to, so that you could be successful. While you certainly know how to plan, you also probably spend a lot of time dealing in the moment. Your day-to-day tasks include executing ideas, putting out fires, solving problems, and fulfilling customers' needs.

I would imagine that the time you would spend planning falls by the wayside on most days. I know I find myself in that boat running my agency, as hard as I try otherwise.

In reality, the truth is that a little bit of planning can go a long way. Now the big brands spend a lot of time planning, probably too much time. They have planning sessions to talk about how to plan. They have teams of people who just sit around planning.

I'm exaggerating, but not by that much. We are not going to go there.

I do want us to think about how to plan a little bit more, though, and a little farther out. All of us already do some planning, at least for the weeks and months ahead, but let's try to go a little deeper.

Let's start by setting some goals; you can't have a plan without a few goals.

Goals are crucial to the success of a brand. As a small business owner, this responsibility falls squarely on your shoulders—you can't delegate it to anyone else. If we don't set some goals, then we really will just be living moment-to-moment, crisis-to-crisis.

So when it comes to planning, the first thing we should do is to set some goals. Think far out: what do we want our business to look like five, ten, or even fifteen years from now? What's the finish line for our business, where do we want to go, and what do we want to accomplish?

Without goals, the brand experience may be purposeless. But with clearly articulated goals, we can make sure that we build a brand experience that accomplishes something specific. Without a plan, we'll never hit our goals, and without goals, there's no way we can do any planning. I know, I'm twisting this all around!

The key is to get past the current deadlines and spend some time planning. Try to get out of what's happening today and this week, and even past just this month or two.

We have to plan a bit in front of us. It's never too early to start planning for next year, anticipating what we might go through and what we want to accomplish. Then I like to say that we should also plan out for the year after as well, just so we can see beyond the horizon. Some goals take a little longer to achieve, and we have to plan ahead to make them happen too.

In a nutshell, I recommend a three-year plan—this year, next year, and the year after that. The big brands call this a strategic marketing plan, which makes it all sound so smart. It's all about prioritizing business initiatives and deciding where to focus.

Like I said, let's start by setting goals. Do we want to:

- Expand the business by entering into a new market?

- Streamline the business by discontinuing items that don't sell well?

- Become the leader and knock a competitor out of first place?

- Dramatically grow revenue by expanding the set of offerings?

- Make better margins by raising prices or cutting costs?

Whatever it is that we want to accomplish over the next three years, write the goals down. Start with the bigger picture, and then get more detailed.

Don't get too caught up in objectives vs. strategies vs. tactics. We marketers always make this mistake. We spend what seems like days debating whether something is an objective vs. a strategy vs. a tactic. Don't waste your time.

Let's get it straight once and for all, at least from my point-of-view, sans the buzzwords:

- Objective: the goal

- Strategy: how to accomplish the goal

- Tactic: specifically what to do to accomplish the goal

Examples always help, so here's one:

- Objective: make better margins

- Strategy: cut costs

- Tactic: negotiate with key suppliers to get better rates

Now this is where the plan comes in, tied right back to the objective (goal), strategy, and tactic.

- Objective: make better margins

- Strategy: cut costs

- Tactic: negotiate with key suppliers to get better rates

- Plan: meet with top three suppliers in the next month to reduce rates by 5%

If you understood that, you are way ahead of many graduating MBAs as they enter fields in marketing. The business may very well have multiple objectives (goals), some bigger than others and some subsets of others. That's great, they can be organized in a logical flow from most important to least important.

The point is to write them down and flesh them out.

As you write out the goals and plan for the business, it's also important to know the history of the brand. Take a good look at what's been working for the business and analyze what is driving the business's success—or lack thereof.

Be honest about identifying the things that are working and the things that are not. Look at each element of the marketing plan to date, and assess whether success or failure was a result. When I was in brand management at Johnson & Johnson, we called this "lessons learned."

Every year, when we wrote out our strategic marketing plan, we would ask ourselves "What did we learn this year?"

So I ask you, "What did you learn this year?"

What lessons have you learned in the past year about the business?

- What kinds of customers are the most lucrative?

- What promotional vehicles sparked the most sales?

- What items sell the best? Why? Did they receive any special promotion?

- What impact did competitive activity have on business?

- What external factors impacted the business the most?

Do an assessment of the employees as well. Which ones performed the best? Which ones impacted the business the most—positively and negatively? Spell out goals for them as well. This falls into human resources more so than marketing, but in many cases the two overlap when it comes to planning and executing a marketing program.

But it's important to know how the employees are affecting the brand's success.

Write down the lessons learned and then match them up with the goals. Take what you've learned and apply it to the plan for building your Experience Effect. Learn from the past to improve the future.

With four or five lessons learned, three or four goals, and a detailed list of strategies and tactics to create, we now have the basis for a very thorough marketing plan. It may not be a one hundred-page PowerPoint deck like the Fortune 500 brands, but it will serve as the basis for a solid look at what to get done over the next three years.

It's great if the plan isn't just "marketing" focused.

The lines are blurred and really anything about the business that needs to get done ultimately is about marketing. Almost everything is a touchpoint, even if one of the goals is to lower employee turnover. Many of those employees are either customer facing or somehow related to marketing.

The truth is that we've been writing much of the plan all along, without even realizing it, through the process we've been going through to craft the Experience Effect:

- Defining the brand

- Identifying the customer

- Understanding the customer

- Positioning the brand

- Mapping out the touchpoints

If we add in annual goals and lessons learned to this list, we will have a solid marketing plan just like the big brands. Our annual goals and lessons learned will make the rest of the plan even more strategically focused and effective. Knowing the goals and what's worked in the past will make defining the brand and understanding the customer even more meaningful.

Surely it can't all get done all at once, so now we have to delineate what we want to get done this year, next year, and what is reserved for future years. We can't get it all done right now, so spread it out over a three year plan. This will hopefully give enough time to maybe even add in a few more goals.

Identify the parts that are best suited for immediate execution from those that can wait until next year, or should really be held off until the year after that. Take each touch-point and put it on a three-year calendar. This will help you allocate the budget and the team's resources to get it all done. If you can't tackle a new advertising campaign this year because of budget concerns, then slot it in for next year. If lowering prices is a major priority, then make sure to start nego-tiating with suppliers this year.

Your marketing plan should be no more than five or six pages, nothing more complicated than that is really required. If it's more work, then it will never get it done.

A focused plan is so much better than no plan at all.

The three-year plan should become a living, breathing document of what the business is all about and what needs to get accomplished over the short and long term. This three-year plan should also include all the lessons learned along the way.

Do this exercise annually, and not only will you have an incredible brand experience for the customer, but a great growth surge for your business!

16

Motivating Your Team
What's On Your Dashboard?

"Align the team around the brand's goals so that they know what they are working toward."

I always say that marketing is a team sport. None of us are in it alone and none of us can do it all by ourselves. It takes a well-coordinated team to pull it all off.

The big brands of course have big teams, so coordinating those teams can be a monumental effort. Your team is probably not quite so big, so it might be a bit easier to keep them all connected, but it still takes a lot of effort.

Now if you are reading this and saying, "but I am all alone," I am going to argue that you are mistaken. Even if you don't have any employees, you still have a team. Chances are you have suppliers or contractors who help you out with your business. They are members of your team too, and you should treat them as such.

Maybe not necessarily the FedEx person, but I'm sure you know what I mean!

In order to create and sustain a consistent brand experience, it's important for all the team members to be on the same page. Everyone should be aligned around what the experience is supposed to be and what the brand is trying to accomplish.

Start with the brand's goals. Be sure to communicate the brand's three-year plan. Align the team around the brand's goals so that they know what they are working toward. Knowing the goal is the simplest and smartest way of accomplishing consistency. At least then everyone is aiming for the same outcome.

Also, share all the information gathered about the customer and the competition. Information not shared is information wasted. Try to keep it simple so that it's easily understood and applied across the entire team. Keep the entire team abreast of all the latest developments and changes in the marketing plan.

Now the big brands use a war room to compile all of this information and to share it. A war room is a place, physically or virtually, where the brand stores all the marketing elements in one location. Some are complete, and some are works-in-progress. The war room is the one place where anyone on the team can access vital brand information. Some call this a style guide as well, which is very similar.

A war room or a style guide basically shares key information about the brand with the entire team. For small businesses, I recommend something much simpler and a little more action oriented—a Brand Dashboard.

The Brand Dashboard is a two-sided document that captures the essence of the Experience Effect that we've been building. It will become the most shared item of your business, and it comes right out of the three-year marketing plan we just discussed in Chapter Fifteen.

On one side is the information that is not likely to change for the year. It should include annual goals, the brand definition, customer collages, key competitors, the positioning statement, and the touchpoint tree. This side highlights the marketing elements in the Experience Effect that we have planned for the year.

As I mentioned in Chapter Nine, the positioning statement is perhaps the most important element. The positioning statement is something that everyone on the team should be aligned around, as well as the other information on side one of the Brand Dashboard.

BRAND DASHBOARD - FRONT

Positioning Statement	Brand Definition
Touchpoint Tree	Annual Goals

Consumer Collage

On the other side of the Brand Dashboard are the metrics of what is happening in real time. It should include current sales, market share, social media numbers, competitive activity, coupon redemption, and any industry benchmarks. It can also include competitive activity, organized onto one page for quick review, and then updated monthly or at least once a quarter to keep it current.

BRAND DASHBOARD - BACK
Current Sales and Market Share
Industry Benchmarks i.e. Sales, Shares, Marketing Activity
Facebook, Twitter, Linkedin, YouTube Statistics
Coupon Redemption History
Competitive Activity

There you have it—the Brand Dashboard. Now it's only going to be effective if we share it with the team.

I'd recommend distributing it monthly and then holding a quarterly meeting with the entire team to keep them on top of what is going on and for each of them to share their roles and thoughts with the rest of the team.

If you can't update the Brand Dashboard monthly, then at least do it quarterly for this meeting.

Get everyone together live and in person once a quarter—it's so important. Do it over lunch, it doesn't matter if the setting is informal. The point is to build camaraderie and to share information so that everyone on the team can be aligned.

You'll be amazed at what it does for team spirit and business results.

You may not have the resources of the big brands, but with careful communication and teamwork you can have a brand dashboard that is just as effective analytically, if not more. The Brand Dashboard will become your most important communication tool to keep the team engaged with the brand's goals.

17 Personal Branding
Be the Brand

"Much of what we spoke about in branding and marketing applies to us as individuals in both our personal and professional lives as well."

I wrote this book to help small business owners cope with the daunting task of marketing their brand. I wanted to impart some marketing wisdom into the process of running a small business successfully, realizing that many small business owners have not had formal marketing training or direct experience.

I truly hope that getting a peek into how the big mega brands do marketing will help.

We just walked through the entire process for creating the ultimate brand experience for a brand, specifically for a small business brand. We took what the big brands do and made it applicable for a small business. We also talked a lot about the importance of setting goals and planning for future success.

You are now a marketer!

I've done a lot of speaking engagements, webinars, and blog posts for my first book. I love taking *The Experience Effect* live and hearing people's reactions and comments directly. Besides getting questions about small business, I also get a lot of questions about personal branding, and how these marketing principles can apply to people as they manage their lives.

Marketing for the real world, you might say.

The truth is that when we do think of brands, we tend to think of the biggies—Tide, Toyota, Marriott, Apple, and Nike are examples, but almost anything can be a brand. Countries, cities, streets—even people are all brands. Yes, people are brands too.

Much of what we spoke about in branding and marketing can apply to us as individuals in both our personal and professional lives.

Think about what actually constitutes a brand. Take Tide as an example. Tide has ingredients—ingredients that take dirt, odor, and stains out of clothes. People have ingredients too—all the skills and talents that we bring to this world.

Tide as a brand has packaging—a very familiar orange package with a blue top. People have packaging as well in terms of the clothes they wear, the house they live in, and even in some respect, the car they drive.

Tide has a very meaningful benefit—it makes mom feel good about taking care of the family with nice, fresh, clean clothes.

Notice the mix of functional and emotional benefits. People have benefits too—all the reasons why other people want to be around each other at work, play, and at home. This is a mix of functional and emotional benefits as well.

Ultimately, a brand is an experience and when the experience is relevant and consistent over time, it has a positive effect on the customer and on the brand. That's true of Tide and it's certainly true of the people that we have in our lives. When the brand is consistent over time, we come to expect certain things from it.

This fact holds true whether the brand is Tide or a person.

I know that is certainly true of me. I have a certain way of dressing (packaging) and a certain demeanor that is generally positive and upbeat (benefit). When I stray from that, people notice. If I wear a solid color shirt instead of my "brand" colored patterns, they ask me if I am feeling ok. If I am unusually quiet and letting others lead, they ask me if everything is all right.

It's so interesting because meanwhile I am just trying out a new shirt or taking a back seat for the day. Nothing's wrong, except that I've strayed from my "brand" for a bit and people notice. They've come to expect certain things from me, including my ingredients, my packaging, and my benefits.

It's important that we recognize this and take action on it. As people and as professionals, we should have a personal brand definition and positioning. We should consciously decide who we want to be and what we want out of life, because then we can make appropriate decisions. We can make choices and take actions every day that affect how people perceive us. The more consistent those decisions are over time, the more successful our brand will become, and eventually people will begin to rely on us more.

This is especially relevant when the personal brand is geared toward a life goal, either personally or professionally. This is even truer when you own a small business.

In small business, it's very difficult to separate the owner from the business. It's often one in the same. I saw it myself when I had my own agency. I was the brand, day in and day out. In fact, it was hard for others to take my place, because our clients wanted them to be my brand too. It's a common "problem" for small businesses but it should be viewed as an opportunity as well.

Often the owner's personality is very much intertwined with that of the business, especially when the owner is the face of the brand (like I was with my own agency).

So it's very important to "be the brand" and to be consistent, a key tenant of the Experience Effect. Live life consistently with the brand you've established for yourself and link it to your small business. Make personal choices that are consistent with your brand, and make personal decisions that reinforce and support the decisions of the business and that will aid in its success.

When you own and run a small business, it's impossible to separate the two brands from each other. Recognize this fact, and be conscious of it.

This is particularly true in social media. While Facebook may seem like it's just among family and friends, how we behave on Facebook can profoundly affect how people perceive us, as we discussed in Chapter Thirteen. Make sure the pictures downloaded and the posts written are consistent with the small business and personal brand established.

Facebook is a permanent public record and it gets shared more than any of us realize.

We need to navigate the digital world, for our personal life, like we would navigate it for work. Sure, we can and should be ourselves; we just need to be consistent with the brands we have created. It can and will affect the business.

We could spend hours talking about personal branding, and it probably warrants another book. Suffice it to say that not only are you a marketer, you're also a brand.

So take it personally.

About Jim Joseph

Jim Joseph is a real-world marketer who has been practicing his craft for over twenty-five years in marketing and sales, on both the client and agency sides of the business, for brands both big and small.

He is an award winning marketing master who has specialized in building customer brands and agency businesses across virtually every consumer category. Jim's consistent goal has always been to help blockbuster clients including Kellogg's,

Kraft, Nestle, Cadillac, Tylenol, Clean & Clear, Aveeno, American Express, Durex, Nexium, AFLAC, Ambien CR, and Walmart create successful brand experiences that engage customers and add value to their lives. Jim was practicing integrated marketing well before it became the buzzword du jour.

Jim is President and Partner of Lippe Taylor, an agency dedicated to "marketing with women" across all categories including beauty, fashion, shopping, food, home, wellness, and even healthcare.

Prior to joining Lippe Taylor, Jim spent the bulk of his agency career at The Publicis Groupe. He started his own agency, which he sold to Publicis and then merged it with two others to create Arc-NY, the largest integrated marketing services agency in Manhattan at the time.

He then went on to Publicis' Saatchi & Saatchi Wellness where he led the transformation of the agency from traditional pharmaceutical advertising to diversified wellness marketing. During his tenure, the agency won several prestigious industry awards including "Agency of the Year" from DTC Perspectives on Excellence, "Most Creative Agency" from The Manny Awards, and a Grand CLIO in Advertising.

Early in his career on the client side at Johnson & Johnson, Jim became a new products expert by launching seven new customer products in less than five years—including the number one Reach Wondergrip toothbrush for kids and the reinvention of Clean & Clear skin care for teenage girls. Jim then went on to become the lead marketer for the Arm & Hammer toothpaste line.

Jim is a graduate of Cornell University and has an MBA from Columbia University. Fulfilling a lifelong dream (aside from writing), Jim also teaches a course in marketing at New York University (NYU), modeled after his first book, *The Experience Effect*.

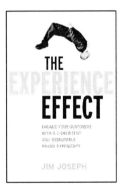

While writing his first book, *The Experience Effect*, Jim found his writing "voice" and he now writes a daily blog about marketing that has quite a following and was also a 2011 finalist as "best blog" from *PRNews*. Winning a silver medal at the 2011 Axiom Business Book Awards for best marketing book is the culmination of that incredible experience.

He is also a regular guest blogger at CustomerProductsGroup.com and RetailShoppingExperience.com. Jim sits on boards of OTC Perspectives, DTC Perspectives, PRSA Counselors Academy, and The Council of PR Firms.

Jim is a frequent contributor to trade publications and is continually quoted in articles for *Advertising Age*, *AdWeek*, and *The Wall Street Journal*. He has done radio interviews for TheMarketingShow.com, ThatAdvertisingShow.com, and Blog Talk Radio to name a few. Jim was also named a 2011 top 100 worldwide business author on Twitter by *Social Media Marketing Magazine*.

Jim lives in Manhattan and Bucks County, PA with his partner of fourteen years and his two teenage children. When not writing his blog or spending time with his family, Jim can be found running along the Hudson River, Lady Gaga in ear!

You can find Jim Joseph every day at JimJosephExp.com.

Other Happy About® Books

Purchase these books at Happy About http://happyabout.com or at other online and physical bookstores.

Red Fire Branding

Liz Goodgold directs her works towards the business-to-business market to help small business owners, entrepreneurs, sales professionals, or anyone who is looking to create an indelible image.

Hardcover $39.95
eBook $19.95

Storytelling About Your Brand Online & Offline

Using this book, professionals and executives of all types, entrepreneurs, consultants, musicians, academics and students will undergo a "personal branding process."

Paperback $22.95
eBook $16.95

42 Rules of Social Media for Small Business

This book teaches readers why social media is important to their business and how they can maximize their social media effectiveness.

Paperback $19.95
eBook $14.95

#SOCIAL MEDIA PR tweet Book01

The tips and guidelines in #SOCIAL MEDIA PR tweet Book01 will get you on the road to understanding the potential of social media for PR.

Paperback $19.95
eBook $14.95

CPSIA information can be obtained at www.ICGtesting.com
Printed in the USA
BVOW022156200213

313811BV00006B/84/P